W9-AZG-604

WHAT IS ARCHITECTURE?

WHAT IS ARCHITECTURE?

AN ESSAY ON LANDSCAPES, BUILDINGS, AND MACHINES

PAUL SHEPHEARD

THE MIT PRESS
CAMBRIDGE, MASSACHUSETTS
LONDON, ENGLAND

Third printing, 1995

© 1994 Massachusetts Institute of Technology

All rights reserved. No part of this book may be reproduced in any form by any electronic or mechanical means (including photocopying, recording, or information storage and retrieval) without permission in writing from the publisher.

This book was set in Melior and Universe by DEKR Corporation and was printed and bound in the United States of America.

Library of Congress Cataloging-in-Publication Data

Shepheard, Paul.
What is architecture? : an essay on landscapes, buildings, and machines / Paul Shepheard.
p. cm.
ISBN 0-262-19341-8. — ISBN 0-262-69166-3 (pbk.)
1. Architecture. I. Title.
NA2500.S47 1994
720—dc20   93-30168
                                                                CIP

CONTENTS

PREFACE

"What is architecture?" is not the same question as "What should architecture be?"

I take my cue from Gertrude Stein's lecture *What Is English Literature,* published in 1935, and E. H. Carr's *What Is History?* published in 1961. Both of these were attempts to explain their subject from a particular understanding, as this book is.

The question itself is old enough, but my understanding is that in 1710, say, or in 1805, the discussions were of a much more contiguous nature than they are now. Then, they used to argue whether the entablature should be Greek or Roman, whether the style should be Gothic or Classic, but now the argument has opened wide. Listen to those voices: Architecture is a metaphor! says one. Architecture is a computer program! says another. It's the voice of the underclass! It's Imagineering!—or is it something on the event-space-movement axis? Can nuclear physics help? Can literature? What questions! What assertions! It's like listening to people fighting dragons in the dark.

My purpose here is not to arrive at a definition for the sake of consensus. In spite of the moves made all around us to limit our understanding to our ethnic boundaries, I think modern knowledge has become far too complex for such an ambition as *consensus*. I would like to frame the possibilities for my subject, however, and so I ask, "What is architecture?"

I would like to thank the many people who have helped me in my search for architecture, most of all Peter Shepheard, Michael Gold, and Jeanne Sillett.

Buck Bourne, Fred Scott, Jasper Vaughan, Fabian Lerat, Robert Harbison, and the late Robin Evans all contributed valuable insights. To Robin in particular, to whom I owe this chance to publish, special thanks.

WHAT IS ARCHITECTURE?

St. George **(C. L. Hartwell, 1936).** Photograph by the author.

1
THE FACTS OF LIFE

In his *Book of Imaginary Beings*, Borges tells us what a carbuncle is. It is a precious stone, a bright red ruby, that is found buried in the brains of dragons. To obtain it, you must do battle with the beast—if not taken fresh, from a living dragon, the carbuncle will dissolve and disappear.

Reports that dragons were still to be found in the jungles of Paraguay sent the Spaniards to South America. They came away with gold, instead, but if you are in possession of a carbuncle, it will give you everlasting fortune and good luck.

THE FACTS OF LIFE

TWO ARCHITECTS

I heard him loud and clear. I heard him with my own ears. I saw him on my own television. I sat in my own sitting room, with the cat snoring like a sphinx in front of the fire, and watched him explain the design of his new building, with its bank of glass-walled elevators running on the outside. *The outside!*

The wind caught his hair and the skyline of the London basin stretched out behind him, from Blackheath to Crystal Palace. They must have been filming on the roof.

"Lifts wear out," he said. He looked like a Roman senator, a wise patrician, with a blue denim toga slung over his shoulder. "Lifts last twenty or thirty years at the most, and the building's going to last a lot longer than that," he went on. He may have looked like Cicero, but he sounded as practical as a vet. "So, to avoid the inevitable disruption that replacing the lifts will cause, we put them on the outside of the building."

The lifts are on the outside of the building to make them easy to replace. That's what he said. I jumped to my feet. I had something to say. There I was, standing in front of the television set, a silent minority of one conversing with thin air:

"What about the escalators?" I said. "Those ranks of escalators that go clear up the center of the building! Won't they wear out as well? What about the disruption replacing them will cause?"

The cat put up her ears at the commotion, though she's too fat and too lazy to move.

"He must have some other reason for putting those lifts there. Why doesn't he come clean?" I said to her.

A child could do it. *We put the lifts on the outside of the building to make them easy to change.* Then what about the escalators! I think children could do this. If this is how we are to argue the points of architecture, then little boys and girls could do it.

Two weeks later, I am sitting in a review of student work at one of London's schools of architecture. This particular class of students shows drawings of brick buildings, one after the other, all the same sort of thing. Red bricks banded with yellow, aping ancient Italy. The professor has been schooling his students on the inevitability of traditional design. He is ruthless, like a dressage master—they call the breaking of horses to the immaculate, unhorselike movements of the dressage *schooling*, as well. The students stand up in front of their drawings and describe what they've done. No *why* or *what for*, just *what*. They don't contribute to the discussion—they remind me of a flock of exotic birds migrating, on their way through, just landed for a short stopover, tired out after the flight. Why not? They've been working all night to get these drawings finished.

Each student's scheme looks the same. *A brick is a brick is a brick is a brick*, I said to myself—and then made the observation, aloud, that a brick is not the only thing to build with—"what about the Assyrian army, who built pyramid trophies in the battlefield out of severed human heads?"

The professor smiles, slowly and generously. He sticks his foot out in front of us.

"Look at this shoe," he says, his voice gentle with care, as if he is describing a rainbow to his lover. "This shoe is made of leather. Leather is a perfect material for the clothing of feet. Leather has been used for centuries for just this purpose. My shoe is made of leather just like the shoes in ancient Rome were. So, bricks and stones have been used for building. They have stood the test of time." He's word perfect; he's said this before.

I'm on my feet again. *Dammit!* The only proper thing to do having jumped to your feet is to say your piece and then walk out. In my mind I have a picture of the planet shooting through space at sixty-seven thousand miles an hour, spinning at the speed of a cruising B-1 bomber, against a huge black background stuffed with things so real but so obscure we can only dream about them. My mouth opens and I hear the words come out:

"Bricks are good if your building is to sit in one spot, being sucked down tight by gravity. But what if you want your building to fly to Jupiter?"—and I actually raise my fist, like Mark Antony on the steps of the senate house— "What then?"

Does that kind of thing get you like it gets me? I call it *the furor*. It seems to me sometimes that we're all sitting in a huge valley with people shouting contradictory things at each other. It's an ancient valley, which was once full of the monuments of civilization; reassuring but constricting. A huge glacier has swept down the valley, scraping it clean, scraping it back to clear rock, and the people are left standing on the rocks, shouting at each other. Free to speak, free to disagree. It's contemporary life, and it sounds like cacophony, because everyone shouts at the same time. Gradually, as each successive argument has been discredited, the floor of the valley has become cluttered with superceded ideas, so it feels, sometimes, that we're up to our necks in rubbish. We cleared the ground of ancient privilege and filled it back up with rubbish. There's the answer, inside the problem—what do you do with rubbish? You clear it up.

I like this analogy because there was a short time that I worked on a street-cleaning gang myself. You have to do something when you write: Trollope got up at five A.M. every day and wrote for three hours before setting off on the business of the day—he was the postmaster general. I used to get up at five A.M., too, and clatter through the streets hurling garbage into the back of the cart, clearing up the rubbish, and then I got down to writing in the afternoon.

Have you ever wondered what it's like, following a garbage truck? Cold and hard and fundamental, that's what. When I started I was fascinated by what people throw away;

I used to try and engage the others in discussions on the merits of relative value. As my brutish friend Steve would say, "What a shithead!" It's a job, not a career—it doesn't matter—it's all rubbish—it's the facts of life. There were four of us altogether, and we all worked with our minds set on the peace of the afternoon to come. We talked, but not to each other, just to the thin air and to our otherselves waiting for us there in the quiet afternoon. It was a strange job, that job—to go with the feeling of limbo there was the howl of the compactor in the back of the cart and the garbage flying through the air and the crash of the trash cans and the bounce of the litter bags—facts of life.

"There's this girl called Cinderella," said Steve one day. He liked to practice his jokes out loud. He had hair three millimeters long, dyed blonde, like a wheat field after harvest. I used to want to set it alight, to burn off the stubble. He always wore a suit to work—a garbage man, mind you—and a collar and tie—and he told smutty jokes all day long. "She wants to go to Prince Charming's party." Steve called this stuff facts of life. "Only telling you about the birds and bees," he said, when we didn't laugh—"only telling you things you know already"—it's cold and hard and fundamental telling facts-of-life jokes as the dawn comes up. "Cinderella wants to go to the party but she can't go because she's got her time-of-the-month," said Steve. "So she calls up her fairy godmother, and says, I want to go to Prince Charming's party but I can't because I've got my time-of-the-month." There's nothing to it, telling jokes the way Steve does. It's like being drunk—staying upright, that ordinary achievement, is suddenly the main thing to concentrate on. He uses words that everyone understands, time-of-the-months, repeats them over and over.

"Oh my dear," he said, putting on the godmother's voice, and he did it mincing toward the pile of garbage bags with one wrist limp and the other on his hip, throwing the words over his shoulder—like a *fairy*, get it? "Oh my dear, we can't have that. Run out into the garden and fetch me a pumpkin." He lifted up a bag and hefted it into the back of the cart and punched the green start button on the compactor like a man conducting an orchestra. He threw the second bag and it flew dead straight and heavy nosed like a cruise missile. "Kerpow!" he said, and clapped his hands together once and grinned at us. "So she gets the pumpkin and she takes it to her fairy godmother. The fairy godmother touches it with her wand and—hey presto!—it turns into"—a slight pause, with his hands forming a vee and his head slightly on one side so he can drop the word delicately—"a tampon." Steve holds up the imaginary article, a tiny little thing the size of a hawkmoth caterpillar, and mimes its insertion into Cinderella's vagina, his own face transformed into hers for one dreamy moment, "Oh thank you, fairy godmother! Now I can go to Prince Charming's party!" He pirouettes and jumps like a ballerina, his suit tails fluttering—it's a lightweight, ten-ounce cloth, even though the day just starting is a winter's day. His face is almost pink, almost grey. The rest of us are carrying garbage bags back and forth across the road, and the truck is grinding along with the compactor roaring in the back, squashing the bags flat like a man stamping out cockroaches on the kitchen floor, *first thing in the morning.*

"So the godmother says, now, Cinderella, remember to be back by midnight. You have to be back before the clock strikes twelve," and I think—this is what I mean by thoughts in limbo—that here Steve is transporting us back to a collective memory that is no longer our experience—he should say, before the *television* strikes twelve. "You must be back before midnight, Cinders my dear," Steve says, slipping into panto language. "So she says, why, godmother? Why must I be back before the clock strikes twelve?" We are shifting rubbish. Steve is doing nothing. He stands on the curb getting ready for the punch line like an orator—*friends, garbage men, countrymen, lend me your ears*—"and the godmother says, oh, Cinderella! You must be back before the clock strikes twelve because that's when the tampon changes back into a pumpkin!"

Okay. It's doubtful. I should be ashamed of myself for even passing it on. But it's one way of illustrating that no two things can exist in the same place at the same time; and to tell you the truth, it doubled us up. We sat on the curb like a quartet of chimpanzees, leaning all over each other, and cracked up. We laughed and laughed and laughed.

Why should I tell you all this? Why should I start a book about architecture called *What Is Architecture?* with tales from the garbage dump? I guess it's facts of life that I want to explain. By *facts of life* I don't mean Steve's patter—I mean real material. You really see it for what it is on a garbage dump—when a thing's broken and chucked out, that's all it is, just material, it loses the value we've added to it with our desires and hopes and ambitions. You can see it clear as day; and now the day itself is another real thing, real beyond narrative value. The thing about it is, when I was doing that trash collector's job I watched one dawn come up after another; I watched the sun rise and felt the motion of the spinning earth. That's the second time I've mentioned the spinning earth inside two pages, and I'll mention it again pretty soon—but don't laugh at me, laugh at Steve. He wants you to. His narratives aren't facts of life, whatever he says. They're like all narratives, loaded with meaning. They have value. They're ambiguous. The material facts—the stones, the trees, the force of gravity—are not like that. They are conclusive. They exist because they exist, not because we subscribe to their meaning. This perception of the facts of life, it's not what I loved about the job—that's just a job, there's nothing to love. It's what I love about humans—what I love about us.

Three Expeditions in Search of Architecture

So what is architecture? Something to do with this material conclusiveness? Part of the answer to the question involves describing the search for it. The question has been asked over and over again, *What is architecture?* Imagine Brunelleschi traveling to Rome with the young Donatello in 1403. I don't know exactly when, I'm a speculator, not an archeologist, but it was around then. Don't look for citations and authentications here—it is enough for me to imagine the man and the youth walking down the road that leads to Rome from Florence, fired with the thought of what they'll find. The ancient stones sit all in a jumble from the sack of the city a thousand years before. I mean just that, piles of rubble of collapsed buildings, which had had their roofs torn out by the Vandals; statues dismembered and thrown in a heap, their ruby eyes gone, lying in mounds of dust, untouched for all that long time. The two Florentines pick their way through the rubble like seagulls on a rubbish tip, *looking for the loadstone.* Brunelleschi finds it. There is a glint of something under a jagged piece of stone, a gorgeous carved head, blind but perfect—*Nobile*—of great and lofty character. *Stones with character,* that's one hypothesis for what architecture is, although it's as primitive as a cave painting to put it so simply. Fillipo lifts the thing into the clear air, his muscles bulging with the weight of it like David hefting the head of Goliath, in triumph: "Ah, Chiero, it is still here."

Young Donatello's eyes bulge at the sight of it, and from that moment he never looks back and through him the trickle of the classical age breaks into a torrent and sweeps away the Gothic—German—*barbarian*—dark ages like a sluice.

This is not my metaphor, this torrent and sluice. It's next to impossible, but I try not to use metaphors when I'm writing. Similes, okay, analogies, better still—but metaphor, isn't that what architecture is? One thing in the place of another? Don't writers use metaphors to borrow the conclusive power of things that exist? And—one more—are not architecture and literature *clean different things?*

As I said, this Renaissance flood of Donatello's is not my metaphor. It's John Ruskin's. He lamented it. In the *Seven Lamps of Architecture,* published in 1849, he writes of Gothic as though it were a miracle, no less than that, a miracle—in whose decay can be traced the downfall of humankind. A glory—*the* glory—that was swept away by the foul tide of the

Renaissance. You could date the end of it, if you felt like he did, you could put a date on the end of architecture—you could write a book called *What Was Architecture?*

Move the scene to a Teutonic forest in 1792. More keen young minds applied to the question, What is architecture? Coleridge and Schiller are trying to figure out where Gothic came from. They know about the classical, but what about this other stuff? The ancient cathedrals, even then four centuries old, glowered down on the neoclassical revival all through its development, so that by the end of the eighteenth century, when the people were cast into deep classical shadows at every turn, the hypernatural levity that the old buildings seem to have, that makes them appear to float over the little towns they stand in, had become an overpowering sensation. The Gothic seemed to represent all the qualities that had been lost in paying too much attention to the mechanics of Rome and Greece.

The two poets stand in the huge black conifer forest and think they can hear Beethoven's music swelling all round them. They come to an abrupt decision: that trees from the ancient forest had been petrified by the coming of the true deity into what we see as columns and vaults in the cathedrals—which were the first modern things in the world. *Gothic columns are, literally, petrified trees!* They saw, in the background of this vision, the pagan ancestors of humanity, gathered round their tree gods, who had dissolved the Roman and Greek stones in preparation for this apocalyptic moment. Back in England, according to Rykwert, there was a man so taken with this idea that he tried to grow himself a

Gothic house, using willow trees: it sounds like the same sort of confusion that Icarus suffered from.

So there's Brunelleschi and Donatello searching through the rubble in 1403. There's Coleridge and his friends enthusing to the skylarks about the petrified forest in 1792. Now here's another bunch of young men. This time, it's in 1932. They are on a pilgrimage in search of *the modern*. They are headed for Paris, to see these tough concrete structures, the Salvation Army building and the Swiss Hostel, both designed and newly built by the immensely persuasive Le Corbusier—a man so persuasive that he signs his letters *the crow* and nobody laughs at him; he charms the girls straight off the sofas just like that, and even their boyfriends are impressed; he says what he likes and sneers at any possibility that he might be wrong. Every opinion he expresses sounds like a conclusion. There is something about the times that welcomes strong leadership: strong doubt, perhaps.

These young men in their tweed plus fours and their *veldtshoen* and their canvas knapsacks on their backs are lucky to have a bright, clear day to see the buildings, so they can see what's meant by *masses in light*. They gaze at the concrete and point and wave at the Swiss students behind the enormous windows, who laugh and wave back and strip off their shirts and flex their muscles like the young heroes they feel themselves to be. The architecture students go back to the Place de Clichy and debate where to go next. None of them wants to go to Florence, that filthy old collection of banker's Palaces. *Those disgraceful monuments to wealth.* This is 1932, this is an age of experiment. Le Corbusier's words are on their lips: "We are embarked on an experiment.

Who knows where it will lead? Perhaps we will fail, but what does it matter whether we fail or succeed? The important thing is that we will have tried!"

"Berlin!" says one of them. "We should go and see Berlin. A new nation is emerging from the ashes of the old."

It happens that one of these boys has a copy of Ruskin's *Seven Lamps* in his pocket. Thrust into his hand by his grandfather on announcing that he was to become an architect. *It's about the same thing,* he thinks. *There's morality in the new building, just like there was in Gothic.* He has only read three of the lamps so far, Sacrifice, Truth, and Power. He's right; it does sound like the new Germany. But there is a confusion. There always is, when people write about buildings. Ruskin says machine-made buildings are deceitful, but modern buildings and machines are wound up together in Le Corbusier's book like a fish and a net. It's no good. Ruskin's little green book with its gold blocked pages condemns itself to its own dark age. The student walks down to the river and stands in the shadow of Notre Dame and tosses the book into the water and watches it float away before turning to face the challenge of the new. So what is architecture now?

——————— FIVE MORE ARCHITECTS ———————

As we all know, the conclusive feeling of 1932 did not last. A lot more water has flowed down the Seine since then. Technology has completely disengaged itself from buildings, when once it was what buildings were. Democracy has changed shape and taken morality with it. America has come to power and found, as the British did in 1902, that the apex of power is the point at which it becomes downhill all the rest of the way—and as the Edwardian British were, Americans are so sentimental about the feeling of ascendancy that was once there that their mouths have filled up with words. What is irony? Why, irony is the sixth level of the theory of modes.

Perhaps it is; for now, I want to say that the landscape has changed since 1932, and on the question "What is architecture?" there is a hubbub, a furor of nonconsensus. It seems to be many things.

Here is a man who scatters chaos on paper and talks about randomness and fractional theory. He calls the scatter the plan of a building. Anything will do—twigs purloined from a pigeon's nest, notes transcribed from the *Song of Songs*—a scribble he did with his eyes shut, like a shaman in a trance drawing in the dust of the Nevada desert. His building is built. It appears like a mirage in the wasteland of the city, a histrionic essay of joints and materials. He claims the building is ambiguous—he says it is like the chaos of modern life—he tells us all that it is profound.

Next to him is another man, building texts. He is very wordy. He remains on site after his building is built to explain the significance of every little piece. There is a metaphysical wind blowing round him, which he explains is spatial too— that everything is spatial. "Look at the distance between the particles of an atom," he says, "is that not space, too?"

Over there is another man. He looks like he's playing with a train set. He is concentrating on working on more and more precise tolerances. His buildings are complex, like the first man's, but they are immaculately ordered. They look like machinery, all nuts and bolts. They are silent like the mountains themselves are—but they remind me of another sort of silence, that of a prisoner on the rack, who knows everything but admits nothing.

Here is a man who's dedicated to rebuilding ancient Rome. His builders think he's a nutcase, who even has to have two-part polysulphide mastics explained to him. They make a bit of a mess of the building, but at least this makes it look old, like it's been repaired, like instant patina.

The last man, most cheerful of them all, plays his poker games with his deadpan, beaming face. "Form has absolutely nothing to do with function whatsoever," he says, thinking, of course, of the modernist maxim saying the opposite, *form follows function.* He says it to wind people up, of course, but what does it make him sound like, a *creationist?* Has he never heard of Darwin? The trouble with discrediting old rubbish is, you just make more rubbish doing it.

Brigitte Bardot (*Le Mépris,* Jean-Luc Godard, 1963). Courtesy of Productions BELA. Photograph from the British Film Institute Archive.

2
ARCHITECTURE IS NOT EVERYTHING

Don't get me wrong—I like those five guys. They are funny guys. Their buildings, as it happens, are all worth a detour. But none of them answers the question "what is architecture?" They have a fix on what it is, a credibility, and so they design the same building over and over, and they talk and write and describe what they do; they use politics and invective and resort to slogans. Their disagreements are played out all the time as though they constituted a discussion.

They all agree about one thing, though. Architecture is their life. They all agree about the fundamental importance of architecture; the central place in the scheme of civilization that it holds. That's what they all say: Architecture is everything. That must be the place to start looking.

So when I say architecture is *not* everything, I mean that there are other things in life, and simultaneously, I mean that there are things that are not architecture, but which fit round it so closely that they help to show what it is.

ARCHITECTURE IS NOT EVERYTHING

———————————— TERRY ————————————

I once worked with a builder who'd spent his apprentice-
ship—when he wasn't taking cars and driving them away—
up on the system-built tower blocks in the East End of London. These were the ones built out of concrete plates stacked
on one another like, it's impossible not to say it, a *pack of
cards*. One day a simple kitchen gas explosion blew out the
wall of one of the flats and the whole stack came tumbling
down like a—well, a pack of cards. Burying people alive in
the rubble.

"You should have seen it!" said my builder, scratching
his belly where his *Games Workshop* T-shirt rode up over it.
He looked like one of those little *Games Workshop* creatures
himself. A snotling.

"You should have seen us." He didn't mean the explosion, he meant the fun they had building the flats in the first
place. He had been up there on the concrete plate floors, with
the crane swinging the concrete plate walls into place for the
men to bolt together and fill the joint afterward with cement
grout.

"You should have seen us," he said. He was balding
and unshaven and crew-cut as well as fat—he looked like a
snotling hedgehog with alopecia. "We had this grouting ma-

chine, it was nothing but a pump and a hose and a bucket of sloppy cement bolted together with a brand name stuck on it. Just an ordinary rubber hose, like the one Elvis used in his trousers. It used to block up quick as an elephant's bathroom, block solid. We never could be bothered to clean the bugger out—we used to stuff the joint with newspapers, instead."

What? All I could think of was those tits-and-ass pictures the newspapers have being scrunched up and stuffed into the joints.

"No wonder the bleeding bolts rusted off, hey?" He licked his lips. "I was not surprised. It came down like a pack of cards. You could not have knocked me down with a sledgehammer when that happened, I tell you," he said, grinning at his glass of beer, getting ready for it. "I was not surprised."

It sounded like a true story, but perhaps I shouldn't have believed him. This is the same man who, two weeks later and without warning, disappeared to serve a two-year jail sentence, right in the middle of the job we were doing. He left me up shit creek with only the baby I was left holding to paddle with—as he might have said.

THE OPERA HOUSE

On the very next day after Terry had been telling me about life building the high-rise, I went to the opera house to see *Capriccio.* It was written by Richard Strauss in the early part of the Hitler war, in Hitler's Germany. It has as its main subject the tussle between words and music—*which is more important in an opera, the drama or the music?* At the end of scene 7 there is a real desert island piece of sublimity, a wonderful orchestral song, that brought tears to my eyes. We were sitting right overlooking the orchestra pit, up near the stage, close enough to see the glitter of ambition in the singers' faces. I watched the orchestra play with a lump in my throat and my cheeks wet in the darkness. I must have looked like one of those Montmartre urchins, all big black tearful eyes and round cheeks shiny in the footlights. I held nothing back—you're supposed to get like this in the opera. I bet even Hitler did. It wasn't just the beauty of the music, though that was as tangible as a fall of snow. It was also the effort the musicians were making to make the performance perfect. To strike every note just so. The conductor was exhorting them with all his heart, and they were really trying, putting every inch they had into their playing. *No stuffing paper in the cracks,* if you get my analogy. I sat there reflecting, aching heart and all, on the comparative performance of builders and orchestral musicians. It struck me then, still seems to me now, that a building is a performance: a one-off, never-to-be-repeated performance where the supervisor is like the conductor and the builders—skilled workers?—are like the musicians in the orchestra.

If the bricklayers and the carpenters and the electricians and the plumbers were trying as hard as the musicians in the orchestra do—that'd be one of contemporary architecture's problems out of the way. But that's not why I mention it. Let's see—the conductor, the musicians. *Furtwangler* and the *Berlin Philarmonic,* and who else? The composer, of course. *Beethoven.* The man who lived in five separate apartments in Vienna simultaneously, five separate apartments, each with a piano in it, shifting from one to the other whenever his friends discovered which one he was living in. Music was everything to him. When he pressed his stone-deaf head up against the soundboard of his piano, he could compose by the feel of the vibrations coming through his skull. Okay, that's composer—conductor—musicians. It works with the drama, too: author—director—players; and so with architecture, architect—supervisor—builders.

Music, drama, architecture, the great arts. Great because they require many people, and great because they correspond to the three states of human existence: facing oneself, facing the other people, and facing the unimpeachable natural world.

KNOW WHAT YOUR BUSINESS IS

Why should I try to discover what architecture is? If it is like music and drama, is it not like everything else? Is not everything like everything else? Is not everything just a part of the great fiction we call real life, an enormous literary phenomenon of interconnected concepts?

Well, no, hell, no; the test for this is to take a gas gun full of cyanide and pump it into a wasp's nest. When the wasps are all dead, take a close look. Is the nest still there? Yes. Do their shelves full of books in wasp language mean anything now that all the wasps are dead and no one's left who understands it? No.

"You must know what your business is," said Gertrude Stein. "There is knowledge," she says, "and there is what you know." This is in the lecture she gave in 1935 called *What is English Literature*. Elsewhere, she points out the fundamental requirement for contemporary life. "The important thing," she insists, "is that you must have deep down as the deepest thing in you a sense of equality." It's good advice to anyone churning round in the apparent chaos of democracy, where nothing is fixed in place and every statement seems to have the same value. *And know what your business is.* Where it starts and where it ends.

There are so many books to read, to find out what architecture is. You might be better off ignoring them and visiting buildings themselves; take a trip to Chartres, get up among the roof spaces at St. Paul's, spend a day riding the lifts at the Lloyds Building. Except that architecture is not just buildings. It may not be everything, but it's not just buildings, it's more than that.

Where to start looking for what else it is? Going into the book stacks in pursuit of architecture is like looking in a butcher's shop for a sheep; it's there, all right, but laid out in a rather particular way. What does someone looking for the woolly animal, the living, undissected entity do? How can I write still more than there is already and risk offering only more chops? Now that architecture is so often explained as having the same ambiguous sense of form as a literary text, how can a person distinguish one thing from another?

I have a suggestion. Don't try to take it all in. Be selective. Start with the first book.

The first book is, in fact, ten books—the ten books of Vitruvius. Vitruvius was a Roman. He lived at the time of the Caesarean expansions, forty years before Christ, in what the old scholars called the Golden Age. They were materialist times. Solid, confident times. I suppose I could have called this book *De Architectura*, as he called his—except that these are not solid and confident times, but breezy times, and my words are not instructions, but more like flags in the wind.

In his book, his ten books, Vitruvius says that the subject of architecture covers three things: buildings, machines, and time pieces. That's why I like the book: I like trilogies, and I think machines are part of architecture, too. Vitruvius says the subject of architecture covers buildings, machines, and time pieces. That's right, *time pieces*.

About buildings, he has a great deal to say. How they are built, what they are for, where they should be. He goes into materials, how to make bricks and different colors of paint, the relative virtues of timber from highland and lowland fir trees. He writes about symmetry, the use of the orders Doric, Ionic, and Corinthian, and the propriety of different designs for different classes of proprietor. How to organize a water supply. All the stuff we routinely discuss now, as it happens—though the orders did submerge for a while back there—when architects get to work on buildings. Of the ten books, eight are about buildings. But, he says, architecture is also concerned with *machines* and *time pieces*. In book ten, he describes the various machines that an architect should know about. Siege machines, they turn out to be; machines for breaking down the city walls he writes about constructing in book one.

So that's *buildings* and *machines*. Now, *time pieces*. Not Rolexes, or Hamiltons, not flip-top hunters in an antique jewelers', not the five hundred years of cuckoo clocks in Switzerland. Not NASA's atomic clock that's accurate to a billionth of a second over a million years. When Vitruvius says *time pieces*, he means *sundials*. Well, of course, architects may as well know about sundials—but why? And why the special chapter?

Think about a sundial you've seen. Perhaps a bronze plate on a stone pedestal, or a bright blue wall-mounted one with gold figures, or a pole in the middle of a lawn with the numbers made out of flowers. Whichever one, it uses the shadow cast by the sun to tell the time, and it's the shadow that's important here. The insubstantial shadow. What the movement of the shadow across the dial shows is the movement of the planet through space, circling the sun—one of the greatest facts of life there is. That's why Vitruvius includes sundials as architecture. And how interesting it is, he wrote, that sundials built in Greece need a different orientation to sundials built in Italy—how interesting, in other words, though he did not know these other words, that the planet spins; and in still other words how interesting it is that we stay located on it not because we are heavy but because we are sucked down onto the surface by gravity. Yes, these are facts all right. There's nothing so certain as these phenomena. It is that absolute conclusiveness, that force-of-nature inevitability, that makes them part of architecture.

I like that expression, *the human condition*. A warm and buoyant sixteenth-century sort of idea. It combines condition in the sense of physical state with condition in the sense of predicament, as well as condition in the sense of contract.

"The condition of life," says Sir Fopling Flutter, "is a hand of cards dealt by fate." Okay—the cards, a geneticist might say, that have been dealt to us by genetic sport, that made us *homo sapiens* in the first place. That enabled us to survive the calamities of the past when the other hominids succumbed and died out, in the *perishing of the unfit*. It is easy to imagine conditions that may annihilate us—climate and disease have replaced the nuclear winter for the time being—but these same conditions might encourage our evolution into something else.

The theory of evolution is a beautiful hypothesis, as cold as outer space. It is a theory of form rather than a theory of creation—it leaves the fundamental question unanswered, *how did life start*, and so humanity is retained, even in its acceptance. Its importance is that it's a theory of form that stands in opposition to the classical one of hierarchy and propriety, pitting the chance of genetic mutation against the neutral, but implacable, forces of nature. It is full of description of chance and change and condition—more useful to us, because of that, to us who want to admit the possibility of change, than the theories of form that depend on staying still.

In spite of this capacity to describe change, the theory of evolution remains a theory of form, not a theory of content.

How does it do it? The dynamic is between the new mutation and the forces of nature. If it were a theory of content, then this dynamic would be reciprocal, and we might call it a context; both object and field would change each other. This doesn't happen. The mutation is a commitment, which is then subject to the tests of absolute forces, and no further changes take place in the individual concerned; if it fails, another mutation of the same genetic pattern will survive. The individual itself does not change. That sounds, to me, like the description of a way of designing architecture.

The holy ones infer, from their comprehension of our minutely intricate selves, that we humans are a miracle of creation, fixed at *point perfect* by God. Evolutionists understand that *we ain't seen nothing yet*—that life will go on increasing its variety toward infinity beyond us, somehow. We are proof of it, even, by our 95 percent genetic commonality with the chimpanzees. Our simple siblings the chimps, who, when it rains, sit there in the downpour trying to keep the ground dry with their bums, with the rain dribbling down their flat faces, all because they haven't figured out how to build umbrellas. Umbrellas? Umbrellas are a mutant form of the desire to stay dry; I think that umbrellas are part of architecture.

This *human condition* is ours, just ours, no other species has it. Farming, politics, and religion are one set of correspondences to the condition. The *great arts* are another: Architecture, music, and drama are responses to the condition. But what is the condition itself? How can it be framed?

First of all, nature. It must be tamed. The terror must be quieted, the land turned to account to profit us. The huge class of things that are not human, from the sunrise to the mountains, from mammoths to viruses, *the lions and the thunder*, everything that cannot speak to us, is what I mean by nature.

I was sitting at a party table once, eating my avocado-and-bacon salad, sipping Warsaw Pact wine, talking to an architect who'd just published his latest building. He had been given a critical approbation that matched his own serious good humor. The building looked like an elephant, gray and fat, that is, with what looked like ivory inlays in the steps leading up to the entrance doors: "the last of the stately homes of England," was how our host described it. What that elephant and England expert Rudyard Kipling would have said about it, I'm not sure. "Very angular," perhaps. Anyway, I was talking to this man, in my best full-purple mode, about nature, about these close-up studies I'd made of praying mantis wings to try and discover an iconography for a scheme I was working on at Christ Church College, Oxford—whose apparently equilateral quad is four feet shorter on one side than the other. I was planning a sort of phase shift of three-meter-tall titanium pins set out in a perfect square inside the quad, and the question was, what shape to make the top of the pins. I daresay you can date the scheme by that description, but my point here is that this architect I was talking to kept referring to God while we were talking about nature, and I couldn't understand why.

"What's God got to do with it?" I said.

"He made it all, of course!" he said—and then, as though I'd said "Really? When? Tell me about it!" he added, "In the beginning. God created nature."

I gave him a black look. My conviction for evolution has made me an atheist, you see, *because I need not believe in God.*

"In the beginning God created evolution," I said, intending to tease this good man a little, but his response was to climb angrily to his feet—I am not the only one who does this—to pick up his plate and his knife and fork, and to carry them to the far end of the table, swapping places with his wife. It was a fair swap. She looked like Brigitte Bardot. I watched her sitting down next to me and thought, *and God Created Woman.* It was the first time I'd ever fallen in love with a married woman.

Now I have stood on the top of a hill in the gritstone heights, with the colors of autumn filling the world beneath my feet with a perfect complementary of red and green, with huge purple clouds underlit by sunlight the color they used to call old gold, and the sky changing from blue on high to orange on the horizon, and gasped at the beauty of it; and what are they evolved from, my two eyes, to be able to comprehend this beauty, if not the substance of the world that looks like this, the rocks and leaves and water vapor themselves? Of course I find it beautiful, I am part of it— that's why it seems to fit me so closely. I lost no time in telling her this—and he, from the other end of the table, thought I was droning on about nature, never realizing I was in fact courting his wife.

So first of all, this human condition, it's nature. Or, to obviate this confusion about creation, perhaps I should start calling it the land. Second of all, as the Texans say, it's the other human beings. All six billion of them. If you were to count one every second, nonstop, twenty-four hours a day, it would take you 190 years; if you were to do the counting with your lover, it would take the two of you your whole lives. You'd need four or five people to do the job between childhood and retirement. To enumerate the other humans, of course, is to suggest a mass of corporeal existence: so much meat. But by mentioning your lover and your friends, I intend to make the point that the second-of-all condition is other people, those to whom we speak and whom we love and hate and whom we act together with. Value is what's important in this second-of-all, since value is how we treat with each other.

I would not be the first to use Robinson Crusoe as an illustration. In *The Educated Imagination,* Northrop Frye attempts to demonstrate that literature is at the center of all things. There is a tendency for other experts besides architects to centralize their activity—I guess it's an indication of the interconnectedness of everything. I have already mentioned John Ruskin's centralization of architecture in the *Seven Lamps.* In lamp number three, Power, Ruskin attributes the fall of Venice to that city's degenerate architecture, to its departure from the proper principles of the Gothic way. In *The Educated Imagination* the literary critic Frye implies that Crusoe proves his humanity by naming the parts of his new world, the sea, the white sand, the coconuts. He brings them into his language, and hence his understanding, by naming them. I would add that Crusoe is shipwrecked by his author to ask two questions: What is civilization? And what, on the other hand, is a human being? And so Crusoe sets about his evaluation of the world, in his case an inventory of everything in it, to make sure he isn't a savage, or, as I would say, to make sure he isn't a chimp.

Now, I would also say that he might, on his own, deal with his surroundings without a word; just moving within the forces of nature—sunup, gravity, electromagnetism, nuclear fission—like the squirrels do, all without a word. He would taste fear and ecstasy, but without a word. As Gertrude Stein says, the great moment of the book, the moment that makes it a masterpiece, is not Crusoe's naming of the parts but his sudden, lonely discovery of another human footprint! Not his own! Which catapults him into a society just like that. With his hair standing on end with anticipation—another human being! *Now* he needs those names. How else will they communicate?

First of all, the land. Second of all, the other people. Now for the third: third of all is ourselves. The emptiness inside us that religion—or creativity—fills up. The abyss inside we face down daily and fill with prayer, or fill with work. The question at the back of all other questions that we answer with faith, or with courage. *What will happen to us?* The tears that spring up and flood us with feeling.

———————————— ANNA ————————————

Anna comes up to me. She is the best student I've had for years. What do I mean by *best student*? Well—she draws like

Michelangelo, she has a sense of passing time years ahead of her age, she turns up week after week with interesting source material that I haven't even heard of. She still finds time to sit and drink and laugh even though she works as hard as a bee. It is Anna who prefers the Gnostic's picture of the world to the theory of evolution. She described it to me once: she said that we are in fact already in hell. Our subjugation to gravity and our never-ending preoccupation with our bowel movements prove it. Our purpose in life, the Gnostics say, since we are already in hell, is to strive for a higher plane, of which there are several. "So this is hell!" I said at the time. "I can deal with this! There's nothing to fear after all!"

This morning, however, she says to me, "I'm confused. I seem to be going in three different directions at once—how do I know which is valid? I've wasted a whole day! I'm so confused."

I say, "You know what the answer to fear is? Bravery! And you know how to stop being confused? Be certain!"

She looks at me as though this doesn't help as much as it sounds like it should, so I tell her about limestone buildings. Close inspection of the stones reveals them to be made of the bodies of solidified animals—what could be more conclusive than that? Unfortunately, she's heard it before. I must have used it in a previous encounter. The good thing is, though, that she has something to tell me—as usual.

"Because a thing is so certain, because it's conclusive and inevitable, that doesn't make it everything," she says. "Architecture's not everything—nothing is."

I invoke nature, *the land,* to illustrate what I mean by conclusive. For this essay, I put it up against two other varieties of meaning. One is the communication between people—ambiguous, imprecise, value laden, and sparking and shorting with the problems of language like an old wiring loom. When a stone is put on top of another stone, the conditions of the land—gravity, weathering, and stability—are certainties. There is nothing to be done about them but to comply. Every exchange of language, however, proceeds on a hypothesis about what the words mean, and something quite different from certainty, ambiguity, is the result. It's beautiful, exciting, productive, meaningful—but not *conclusive* in the way that landed things are.

As for the third—the self: I think that meaning within oneself is neither conclusive like the land nor ambiguous like language, but something else again. *Revelation* is the word we have for it, though revelation as a word is a landed metaphor, as in a curtain drawn aside. But it means a sudden comprehension, like that moment of perfection I realized at the opera house, the beauty of human effort, which wrenched tears out of me—it means understandings that are achieved *beyond words,* as Brigitte Bardot might have said. It's not a complicated matter, this—it reads simply because it is simple.

When I mentioned the great arts of music, drama, and architecture, with the little structure of composer, conductor, and musicians, it was a classical figure. It was static. It served its purpose, but now it needs to become the vehicle by which I separate three kinds of meaning, still in the pursuit of what kind of meaning architecture has.

Expansion is what the figure requires. Art is everywhere. As life has become detached from the wilderness, the human world is everywhere. I see music as a throbbing accompaniment to every moment of contemporary life, a sort of continuous current of emotion, that incorporates what poetry used to be. I see drama as a hugely expanded art that includes films and novels, which even has a new name, literature, and sucks in clothes and manners to itself as well. Architecture? Would we not all agree that architecture is much more than tombs and palaces and temples now?

Do you remember those stories that ended "and the moral of the story is . . ."? The first definition of moral is *meaning*. Morality, if you can forsake the absolute sense of something handed down from on high, is another way of describing the results of human discourse, of describing the trust between human beings. Literature is full of that sort of meaning. Music is like the self, full of revelation. What about architecture? Architecture is like the land, conclusive. And what about all the ambiguity that is promoted in architectural design, at this moment in time? Exactly—a contamination by literature. No two things can exist in the same place at the same time. They may *look* as if they do, but that's not the same as being.

If a spatial entity can be only itself—cannot physically be something else at the same time—what is the nature of that phenomenal complexity that surrounds us? What is that multivalence that buildings have, for example, which is so often construed as ambiguity? The books in my library are all arranged on shelves at head height. They are full of ideas, especially the ones that are full of definitions. One day I was searching for this word, multivalence—*many degrees of valency*—and so, valency—*valient, forceful*—and so, because it was there, Valencia—*a cloth of mixed material, silk, cotton, and linen, usually striped*—ah! different strengths woven together, to make one thing!

The sunlight boomed in through the curtains. The music was *Pelleas and Melisande*, not Debussy, but Sibelius, good and loud, as ecstatically sentimental as a walk along the cliffs. I was singing along to it. There on the shelf next to *Multivalence—a Book of Definitions* was John Summerson's book *The Classical Language of Architecture*.

"What's this?" I sang aloud, "language and architecture? And are they not *clean different things?*"

No one writes in English like Summerson. We try, but we don't. So what was I to make of what seemed to me to be confusion, confusion in the house of the master? I might just have read in Shakespeare that women were not worthy of men's love! In *The Classical Language of Architecture* the armature analogy is grammatical. *Latin Spoken Here*, says the sign on the door. But of course Latin is spoken nowhere; is a dead language any more a language than a dead donkey is a donkey? Is a dead language not more like a set of spaces laid out like a maze? What struck me when I read Summerson's book is that his actual analogies are hardly ever literary. Character, gesture, proportion, for example; these are words we use for things that stand in space. Besides, his armature of grammar is nothing compared to his wonderfully precise perception and the clear humanity of his prose. This all only matters to me because it is Summerson himself, elsewhere, who explains what the multivalence of a building is to us: by describing a facade as a *continuously related set of inventions*. A clearer, more efficient phrase would be hard to find, with all five words fully active, fully descriptive, and essential.

—— LANDSCAPES, BUILDINGS, MACHINES ——

I once went up to Hull to talk at a student's conference. It's a hard place, Hull, thinly spread, and built on the banks of a huge, cold estuary. The students were up in arms about *the cuts*. Three or four schools of architecture were going to close because of the financial cuts, and they wanted the Rot-Stopped-Now!

The lecture hall up there has one of these steep rakes of seats, like the operating theaters in old hospitals, built for spectators to watch the body being cut up. I started my lecture in my usual fashion of that time, with a little story about Abe Lincoln's Gettysburg address. It's a speech about the moral purpose of the Civil War. "Four score and seven years ago our fathers brought forth on this continent a new nation, conceived in Liberty and dedicated to the proposition that all men are created equal," it starts. "That government of the people by the people for the people shall not perish from this earth," it ends. Well! The point of my telling the students this is not to rouse a cheer for democracy but to point out that this famous speech takes only two-and-a-half minutes to say; that during that two-and-a-half minutes, the audience takes in nothing, because it is adjusting its ears to the cadences of the speaker's voice; that Lincoln spoke his words among other men's speeches about revenge and the sin of rebellion, which was what his war-struck congregation really wanted to hear. It is as though he knew his words would not register with the angry people in front of him, and so he put them in a time capsule—two-and-a-half minutes—and lobbed them into the future, when peace might have a chance.

To say all this of course takes about two-and-a-half minutes, so now the audience can hear what *I* say, so I start on the lecture proper, the good old White Horse of Uffington Down—when someone stands up at the top of this huge cliff of seats and says, "We don't want to hear about Gettysburg—or the White Horse—or what you think architecture is—we want to hear about *the cuts.*"

I was caught off guard. "Well," I said, "I've been traveling round architecture schools giving talks like this for the last four years now, and wherever I go students tell me how rigid their courses are, how irrelevant their projects are, how lost in the wilderness are their tenured staff—" I leaned forward and took a breath, "Perhaps it's no bad thing they close the schools."

I was insulted—*Thatcherite*—reviled—*middle class*—marginalized—*white male*—but I sat there and took the flak and drank my way through forty centiliters of whiskey until the activists had left and two-thirds of the audience still sat there, saying, "Tell us about the White Horse—*please!*"

Now, one of those who stayed behind introduced me, in the discussion that followed, to the landscape theory of Jay Appleton, professor of geography at Hull. Multivalence comes up again here. He said that our pleasure in the field is located in the pleasure associated with our mechanisms of survival. "Look at that cave," he said. "It is at once a refuge and a terror—a safe place to hide, that is, unless something nasty is hiding there already." He called this mixed feeling *ambivalence,* and attributed it to the cave itself; a notion so close to *ambiguity*—which I kept saying the land just doesn't have—that when I first heard it, woozy as I was, late at night, with the rest of the whiskey inside me—when I heard it, this *ambivalence of the landscape,* I felt it rock my boat. Until I realized that it is something else, *multivalence,* a thing of many strengths, that he was comprehending. It is either a cave with a bear in it or an empty cave—the fact that we can't see through rocks should not obscure its essential clarity.

Where Summerson solved my complexity problem, Appleton added this particular understanding that we like things—find pleasure in them—because they are related to our survival. Humans have evolved by finding pleasure in what they must do to survive. Sex, eating, problem solving, exploration, knowing. So what do I like? Is it important? Don't tell me that *taste* comes into it, too! Well—taste is vital; it is taste that identifies the poison in your food.

The landscape that contains our hopes and fears, I think, is part of architecture; the subject is wider than Appleton says, and the perceptions of it are more varied than he suggests. Architecture is not everything, but though it is not everything, we must include in it everything that it is. Architecture is the art of the land. As art, it is the manifestation of the human perception of the land.

Let me take you back to Vitruvius for a moment. He said architecture consists of buildings, machines, and time pieces. By "time pieces" it turned out that he meant the huge spectrum of the earth and the planets—as indicated by sundials. There is a scale of things all to do with *the land,* at one end of which are the forces of nature, the perception of which, at any given place, I would call *landscape.* At the other end of the scale are the local difficulties solved, and the opportunities opened, by our use of machines—and somewhere in between are the buildings, which, if conceived grandly and accurately enough, can extend outward to embrace each end of the scale. Landscapes, buildings, and machines.

***We Are Making a New World* (Paul Nash, 1918).** Photograph from the Imperial War Museum, London.

3
DÉBUT DE SIÈCLE

What has happened? Why has *architecture* come to mean only *buildings*? Why do some architects try to copy machines while others try to ignore machines altogether? Why do architecture students fall in love with mystic practices? And most of all—why does architectural theory these days sound like literary theory? To have even a chance of answering such questions, we must go back to the start of the century: to the time when everything started to become invisible.

DÉBUT DE SIÈCLE

SALLY

I eat sometimes at a café that has tables on the outside, on the pavement. Because it's London and not Paris, this is *unusual,* and so the traffic intrudes its noise and smell right in among the ketchup bottles and sugar shakers in the middle of the table. Right in among the bacon and beans on the plate. I was having lunch with Sally there one day. Sally, who has a mind of her own. She had returned to the city recently as a refugee from the country—where she had gone as a refugee from the city ten years before, specifically to escape discussion with her neighbors about *what car she should get next.* "So shallow and consumerist—as if it should matter what sort of car I got next."

She had gone to a two-field smallholding in Norfolk to get away from all that, and she knew it was time to leave when one of her ex-urban neighbours came round for a chat. "And you know what he talked about? Nonstop? What sort of pig to get next." Before that happened, however, she had lived country ways, she had had children, worn aprons, stayed up all night watching glowworms, and finally she had become a carpenter.

"I bought this stock of oak from a man in Tivetshall St. Margaret," she said, stirring her coffee with those eczema-troubled hands of hers. She was so tense! "All the villages round there have the name of the church appended to the name of the village. God knows why." Big smile: little-girl-wide-eyed smile: "Well, He probably does."

I like watching Sally talking. She talks like someone from Manchester. Her whole face moves, her eyelids, the groove in her chin, her cheek muscles, they're all in use the whole time.

"I had three hundred and sixty-five oak boards, six feet long. Still lively, still green, six-by-ones. When I got them home, well, he delivered them in a huge red tractor, the kind with front wheels as big as the front? Four wheel drive?"

"Murder the subsoil," I said.

"They *don't*. I *asked* him about that." She drew her face into a flat white board, hostile, and clenched her fists, and then suddenly relaxed. It was like watching a cloud shadow racing across a hillside. "You're teasing me. God, they don't tease in Norfolk. They needle, but they don't tease."

"The wood," I said to remind her. "The oak."

"Yes. We unloaded it and I laid the boards out all over the field and closed my eyes and held my hand out like this—" she put her hand out horizontal, fingers flat, four inches above the table. "I could *feel* them!" she said.

"Feel?" I said. "Feel what?" and she laughed at my poo-poo expression and shook her bangles at me.

"Feel the *emanations*." She has black hair and blue eyes, an unusual combination, but just then it looked like an Ad Exec's cliché.

"Jesus, Sally, you're ridiculous," I said.

Still—she went on to explain how she could not only feel the emanations but had sorted out her oak boards into piles on the basis of these emanations; and still further, she had made several tables in which the oak boards were graded, from one sort of emanation to another.

"It was invisible, yes?" I said. "You couldn't tell—I mean *no one else* could tell that the boards weren't the same. No one else could sense this pattern." She smiled and winked. "The boards were all the same, Sally," I repeated.

"My god, look at that bus!" she said. "Look at that red." I looked—the big red thing moved slowly past like a troopship and we watched it go, reliving childhood: "A bus! A bus!"

"It's because it's red," said Sally. She suddenly grabbed the ketchup bottle and held it up to my face. The label had been soaked off by the café owners, so they could reuse it. It could have been a bottle of blood. "Look at it! Look at it!" she said, urgently. I looked at it and she moved it sharply to the left. My eyes went with it. I couldn't take my eyes off it. "There!" she said, "You couldn't take your eyes off it, could you?"

I still don't know whether Sally's crazy or not. She's better company when she's drunk, when all this cosmic stuff gives way to a sort of deep liquid hum of pleasure—but there, in the sun, on the sidewalk, with the trucks hurtling past crashing down into third gear for the ascent of Highgate Hill, she suddenly made good sense. She sat there calmly eating her bacon and beans and explained to me how she had read, in German, Goethe's color theory—Goethe! The great poet and friend of Beethoven! She said his color theory includes this can't-take-your-eyes-off-red, and also the notion that every time you have an idea there's a flash of yellow behind your head, a little to the left. Remember those cartoons with light bulbs in thought bubbles meaning *idea*? That's where they come from. There's some sublime animal character in this theory that helps to explain something. Not architecture, perhaps, but maybe Beethoven. That's as precise as I can get, because I'm not as crazy as Sally. I don't confuse ideas with space.

What relevance has all this got to my question, What is architecture? I think that it's about things being invisible but still having character. I think of it as a very modern theme— not inevitably contemporary, perhaps, but modern. Le Corbusier, in *Vers une architecture*, says, "Day by day our epoch is defining its own style. Our eyes are yet unable to see it." And never will, I think, it's invisible. If we see anything, it'll be the side effect of something else.

—— A SHORT HISTORY OF MODERN LIFE ——

At this point I am going to insert a much-rehearsed piece. It's a sort of short history of modern life, with an emphasis on technology. It takes the form of an analogy, in which the gates of an old city are flung open and all the people spill out into what had previously been considered the wasteland outside the walls. There was a time, I've been told, I guess before 1700, when travelers going from one place to the next by coach would pull the blinds down to blot out the wild and hostile nature they were passing through. No question of the scenic route for them!

What does my short history of modern life sound like? First, it would reach back and touch as a base the date 1789, for the sake of the enlightenment and rational democracy. Liberty! Equality! Fraternity!—however an unstable trilogy that is, with each of its terms tending to cancel out one of the others—is a world away from the mystical rationalism of Newton, two generations before. Newton's notebooks reveal the effort he made to come to terms with Old Testament descriptions of the forces of the beast and the forces of heaven: his fields of study being, on the one hand, gravity, on the other, light. These are two profound, architectural subjects, to which St. Paul's Cathedral is a monument, but my short history of modern life is a history of escape from such monuments. Starting in 1789, my history would touch the date of the *Origin of Species,* 1859, and also on that fine Russian nihilism of the same period that wanted to *clear the site*—sweep all the rubbish away so a new start could be made. Then it would set the years of the first decade of this century for its major action. Imperialism fatally wounded by guerilla war in South Africa, 1902. Rutherford splitting the atom for the first time, 1903. The first powered flight, 1903. The publication of the *Special Theory of Relativity,* 1905. The first exhibition of cubist paintings, 1907.

"Bliss was it in that dawn to be alive!" said Wordsworth of the French Revolution—he who sold out with all the others, leaving only poor Hazlitt—according to Hazlitt—to champion Liberty! Equality! Fraternity! and bliss must it have been as well in Paris in 1905. The start-of-the-century events I mention indicate the possibility, at last, of an actual people's democracy that for two centuries had been in preparation— a democracy where everything is relative, where machines do the work, and where science sets the pattern for society— *experimental*: but then right on top of all this ferment came the bloodiest war that has ever been seen. Ordinary men, civilians in uniform, walking into machine-gun fire. It must have felt, after that, that the ground had indeed been swept clean.

That's the action set. The scene is the central figure, this ancient city, where everything was fixed and hierarchical and brilliant; lustrous, though stained with filthy privilege. It's the sort of place *Cinderella* is set in—people know their place, it's the king's word that goes. You cannot help yourself; finding a prince is the only way out. You have to put up with his father, too: it was that old man's scheming ingenuity that made his son coat the steps of the ballroom with tar that night, in an attempt to trap the girl, like a bird trapped by lime; only her slipper stuck, however.

They all lived in this brilliant, lustrous though *stained* city stuck like this, until events conspired to show the people how to get out. They sensed a greater world beyond that in which they had been instructed. They rose up and tore down the gates.

Now when the gates of this city were finally torn down and all the people rushed out into the sensual wilderness that the walls had been built to overcome, and when they found that all the material of the world and all the shapes of the world and all the life, too, could be the subject of perception, not prescription—each one's own perception, that is, true to what was really seen and really felt—why, what a babble was on! When everyone suddenly has the freedom to speak, they all speak at once and it sounds like cacophony! Only the *abstractions* could shine through the clamor.

Most of all, technology escaped the immovable tyranny of buildings and slipped its leash to join the dramatic whirlwind. The time of the ancient city was a time when everything was like a building. Whereas before this time the people had been fixed in their relation to each other—king, noble, yeoman, serf, just like the prune stones round the edge of a plate—and buildings themselves had been the model of society, a building being the perfect expression of a set of fixed relationships, *conclusions* in my earlier term; from this moment, with the gates of the city broken down and people swarming out over the wasteland that surrounded it—wasteland, that is, because it's wild nature, uncultivated—the great current of human preoccupation shifted from architecture to literature. *Other people, not the land.*

CONRAD

That's it—my short history of modern life. I remember the time it first came to me, this image of the gates of the city sprung open, and all the people swarming out into the wasteland, noisily arguing their heads off about every new thing that came up. I had been to see my old friend Conrad—I call him the old man of the armchair—he is the oldest, wisest being I know. He is so old his body has almost given up on him. He sits in his armchair all day long looking as thin and brittle as a pencil, except for his huge wise head lolling on his chest. He shakes, gently, all the time, which even though he's almost dead makes him seem more alive than anyone else in the room. He has to fight for it. He has to grab the arms of his chair tight, as tight as he can, to stop his old self from sliding onto the floor. When I sit and talk to him, I can see his bones shining through the skin of his fingers, and I am conscious of the weight of his wise old brain pressing down on the bones of his neck. When I went to talk to him and tell him about evolution and being an atheist because of it, he made me feel like a baby.

"Atheist? Confirmed atheists are always such bloody fools," he said.

"I'm not like other atheists," I say, "I believe in faith and prayer."

"How's that?"

"I need faith to answer the great unanswered question, Why are we here? But I don't call it faith, I call it courage."

He looked at me with his eyes glinting, wondering, I suppose, how I could talk about courage, who never yet faced death—as he does, daily.

"What do you call prayer?" he said.

"Prayer is another name for work."

"And what will you do when you lose the strength to work?" He opened his hands out to show me the enormity of it and clutched the empty air with his feeble fingers. "You lose your strength, you know."

But, you beautiful old thing, I thought, you do stay useful.

The next time I went to see him, I went with a purpose. I figured I was doing him a favor by making him useful. I wanted to see how he could help reshuffle the pieces of my short history of modern life into a proper suit—he had lived through it, after all. I took Sally along with me, to soften him up, and it was a good move: she walked straight up and kissed his cheeks and shook her black hair at him and filled the room with pungent life. In no time he was wide awake, his memory blazing like a gun, telling us all about it. His birthday, he said, was on armistice day.

"I was five years old exactly, on November the eleventh, nineteen eighteen," he said, throwing his voice at us like an actor. "I woke up to the sound of churchbells: every bell in the country was ringing to celebrate the end of the war. But of course I didn't know that—all I knew was, it's my birthday—I thought they were ringing all those bells for me!"

Sally laughed, and clapped her hands, and I sat there like the next generation, waiting for the baton to be passed. Ask him about Le Corbusier, Sally, I thought. That was why we were here.

"What about Frank Lloyd Wright?" said Sally. "Did you ever meet him?"

"Yes, I did—I met him in a Knightsbridge mews in the summer of thirty-three," he said. He was almost singing to her. "I don't know how we managed it. We were students— poor as churchmice—" he flicked his eyelids slightly to indicate a parenthesis coming up—"It's the proper state for a student. Too much money turns one toward the main-stream—the mainstream is a current too strong to think in."

While Sally nodded her head emphatically, Conrad's housekeeper appeared, carrying a tea tray with a brown pot with a knitted cosy on it. The old man went straight on with his *poor as churchmice* reverie, looking all the time at Sally, while I started pouring out the tea. "One of our chaps used to make up a vat of porridge—huge black saucepan full—and pour it into the top drawer of his desk, and let it set overnight. An ordinary wooden desk. His breakfast was a slice of this cold, stiff porridge—every morning he opened the drawer and cut off another slice! And ate it!"

He seemed to have shed his age. He had let go the arms of his chair and his fingertips were pressed together in front of his face and his eyes twinkled away at Sally like a mountain stream. Sally reached out and touched his arm and laughed with him about the porridge—"so that's what kitchen drawers are for!" she said, and rattled her bangles at him so he would notice the beautiful hairs on her arms—"but what about Frank Lloyd Wright?"

"Ah yes. Frank Lloyd Wright. Somehow we had persuaded both him and Le Corbusier, the French architect—the two great men of the moderns, so we thought then—we had persuaded them both to come to a party in our tiny place in Knightsbridge. It was just a small room—the size of this study, twelve by twelve—and everyone had come, all us students and our girls, and the two great men, all squashed in—and they refused to even acknowledge each other's presence! They were so jealous of their reputations that they refused to talk. They stood back to back in the middle of the room—one facing the fireplace, the other facing the window, each spouting forth the future, and each with a circle of admiring young faces round him—and they never even looked at each other once."

"Wow!" I said, passing out the teacups. "That must have been noisy."

Sally and the old man looked up as though they had forgotten I was there. It served me right. I'd gone to exploit his memory, to be a tourist, not a pilgrim. I deserved to be looked at as though I were a machine.

Anyway, that's when I realized why the wasteland is noisy. Having embraced liberty, the people, no longer subjects, start arguing. The arguments wind up and up—they're never supposed to end. Consensus is a mirage, for the fainthearted. *The arguments are not supposed to end.* This is liberty, and everyone has a right to speak.

The Russians set the pace, they severed their lines with one sharp blow. They designed buildings made of abstract shapes, leaning forward *into the future.* They proposed the destruction of the city of Moscow, with the people, volubly debating, spread out over the surface of the earth. Without the constraint of the Tower of Babel, you see, the multitude of voices can be borne. They composed music for factory hooters, played by orchestras without conductors. They invented Sobotnik!—which was a working Saturday when a man worked for nothing, as a contribution toward the common good.

"Wait a minute, orchestras without conductors?" says Sally. "Is this like architecture without architects? Or the drama without an author?"

It's another confusion, since both those things have been lauded, iconoclasticly. As I said, I think my architecture-drama-music comparison served its purpose in suggesting the land, the people, and the self; the *grand art* epithet is a classical notion, perhaps of little currency. Instead of Beethoven, Shakespeare, and Alberti, for example, one might for the wasteland say *people, people, and people*. Tommy, Ivan, and GI Joe. Individual or general? It is in this way that the drama has been transformed into literature. By Defoe, say, and that well-known individual Robinson Crusoe. There's the start of the confusion, right there. Literature, though it includes everyone, includes them all as individuals, not as citizens. It is a more singular idea than the drama, with lonely readers wrapped in private thoughts instead of taking part in citizenship together down at the theater, which is in itself analogous with the double-edged offer of liberty: "You're free, aren't you; work it out for yourself!" At the same time literature can nose its way in anywhere, take in anything to itself, by its overwhelming mastery of the content. By comparison to what I mean by literature, and although the subject is all still people, people, and people, Shakespeare's dramas are fixed in place, as full of metaphor as a brick building is full of bricks, and as closely fitting to the theater they were performed in as citizens were to the city—before they became liberated and went to dwell in the wasteland.

For hard-line liberals, everything is relative. Everything is a hypothesis. This piece of writing is such a thing. It's a moral

Primitive peer pressure

The Far Side ®

March

1493
Spaniards report that the people in the New World "drink" smoke. It is Europe's first contact with tobacco.

Thursday 9

- 4 ?
- 9 ?
- 11 ? —last; Gary read it? anyone?
- 13 ?
- 15 ?
- 16
- 21
- 23
- 25
- 38

- 67
- 68
- 75
- 76 ?
- 77 ?

- 46-48
- 50-51
- 57 ?
- 60
- 61-62

48
51
67

matter, not a *landed* one: it's about how people can live together, and about what they can agree on. "What is architecture?" is a question of definition. It's literature that grapples with these questions. Literature can cope with the fluctuation and the revision and the ambiguity, because it's like that as an art. A piece of architecture cannot be ambiguous, because space is exclusive. No two things can be in the same place at the same time. Try clapping your hands together. A building that claims ambiguity can only do so by illusion, like a conjuring trick.

"What about that building in Farmagusta which is a mosque and a cathedral at the same time—a hall of columns oriented to Bethlehem that embraces a nave oriented toward Mecca?" Precisely. The ambiguity is in the name of the thing. The literature. The thing itself is just what it is, a matrix of columns at one orientation with a space set in it a few degrees off line. That's the *landed* description.

So, while Conrad and Sally chatted and flirted, I sat back and sipped hot tea and thought about how our attention is diverted by a mirage of consensus as we wander further from the city walls into the wasteland. At these great distances, with the domes of the shopping malls glinting in the sun, we have only our machines to rely on. Buildings are no longer in the van of our engagement with nature. Look at them— they idle, trying to be included in one way or another. Perhaps by being like literature, even—being *meaningful*. Perhaps by copying the machines—being *useful*. Perhaps by being like bank notes—*worth something*.

There Was a Time When
—— Everything Looked like Buildings ——

The land never disappears. The exploitation of it changes. In that walled city, the building was the sum of technology. The apogee. Everything that could be done was done in building. Look at the effort given to roofing the transept of Santa Maria del Fiore, in Florence, and at the same thing done again at St. Paul's in London. In Florence, Brunelleschi invented a double dome, the inner supporting the outer as they both were built. With this practicality went humor: he incorporated wine and bread shops into the space between the two domes for his masons, to rub in the fact of their great and inaccessible height from the ground. Brunelleschi told jokes as heavy as hammers. He once had to scold a student for getting the architrave upside down on the Innocenti.

"But master, I copied it from the Baptistry."

"My boy, the Baptistry is indeed wonderful. There's only one thing wrong with it, and that's the architrave."

Brunelleschi won the job for the dome in a competition. Another suggestion had been to fill the transept with a mountain of soil and stage a scaffold off that.

"And what of the expense of removing the soil?" asked one of the committee.

"We mix the soil with gold coins," was the answer, "like the Emperor Hadrian did at the Pantheon. The workers will cart it away for nothing."

The dome at St. Paul's is even more extraordinary in its virtuosity—but I'll describe that later. This technology I'm describing here, this way of looking, this way of framing thoughts, this is all buildings. Throughout the long neoclassical period everything looked like buildings. Everything fixed in its relationships with everything else, just like a building. Stage coaches, clocks, crinolines—those armatured hairdos in *The Rape of the Lock*. That Royal Society pair of globes, the earth and the moon, with their fluted, Corinthian columns. The serving tables with a frieze the same as the dado rail, and the carpets that mirror the ceiling patterns, in an Adam house. Even the ships, with a long history of technical specialty, had columns and sash windows in the captain's quarters at the stern.

A short history of things might show the cottage of technology to be tied to the Renaissance palace. In those days, flight was just a myth, with Icarus chancing his feathers in the sun and crashing to his death amid hoots of laughter. The bonds were kept tight right up to the time when precision flowered, and the planes first really flew, and technology became free—just like us.

──────── THE ESCAPE OF THE MACHINES ────────

There is an art of *worldly matters*, distinct from *spiritual matters* or *conceptual matters*, whose kingpin has become what is meant by architecture now—building design—but which includes other things. Not everything; just those things that are manipulations of nature, of conclusive physical facts. Funeral pyres, drystone walls, and telescopes all fit, for example. There is a specially active group of things, with limited dedication but with effects out of proportion to their size: machines. The machines, which in Vitruvius's book are simply dedicated to building or destroying buildings, have now come into their own, and I've suggested that we may track the cause to the social liberties that have been fought so hard for. Machines are expedient, thorny, opportunistic. They nose out the corners of a modern individual's life just like literature does: they manage to do it by compromising with time and lasting only as long as they need to.

The biggest change came when they pulled away from the mother art entirely and went subperceptual. Became electromagnetically biased, dependent on sophisticated calculations at computer speeds, beyond the scope of human hands. As likely to be gold-plated for utility as for decoration. Becoming smaller and smaller, affecting nonspectral black in order to further obviate the senses.

Technology minimizes local difficulties in pursuance of the good. The machines have proliferated to minimize more and more localized difficulties; in the end, the consensus of civilization, from the bloody exhilaration of being gathered in the Colosseum in Rome, via the glorious two-hundred-year-long building programs of medieval Europe, to the nice judgment of concert hall audiences in Vienna, all that civilization, is traded for the permutation of a number of technologies that, taken together, constitute a way of life. Who can say that this is not beautiful?

Meanwhile, the arguments—the furor—about value rage on. It seems like chaos, like overload. The primary responsibility of the contemporary citizen caught in this maelstrom is to be selective; the second is to stand up and be counted.

———————

Here comes the shuttle orbiter *Columbia,* gliding in from space toward Edwards Air Force Base as silently as the *Santa Maria* herself. Its undersides are as black as a bomber's. To withstand the heat of reentry, the ship is covered in sublimely expensive ceramic insulating tiles, stuck on with some sublimely sophisticated glue. Known as *conformal* tiles, their shape is defined by the aerodynamics of the hull: not one of them is the same shape as any other. There are no procedural economies here; this is desire-led technology, this technology is as high as a kite. But the real point of the analogy, in this glimpse of the shuttle, technology like some huge overgrown cuckoo chick, is that following the big ship is a tiny T38 chase plane, its cameras whirring, and its occupants, two excited observers, are chattering their helmets off to mission control. The pipit to the shuttle's cuckoo.

That old crow, Le Corbusier, from a different vantage point— the driving seat of a Bleriot monoplane?—made his observation of the age defining its own style. He set out in his chase plane in pursuit of an event of real significance—space shifting, antigravity, time-warping significance—the escape of the machines.

It is amusing now to look at the illustrations of machines he chose for *Vers une architecture.* The echo of the everything-looks-like-buildings stage is still there—the ships look like palaces, with their upright funnels. The cars look like stage coaches, with their open seats for the drivers and their *Brougham* and *Landau* fittings. But they are changing fast, changing year by year, becoming themselves. The buildings that are supposed to match the machines' intense zest for the task at hand are nothing like them. It's as though they have been stunned into neutrality. Quiet, ordered, flush, cleaned of all ornament—their plans like stately homes with the grand staircases taken out so that *everyone*—the people— has to use the servants' stairs. Democracy!

For the architects of that time to see the machines slipping away from buildings and starting to explore the liberated world, nosing out areas of more and more local specificity, even while the painters were starting to explore their liberated perceptions—it must have been hypnotic. No wonder they felt like chasing this enormous potential, felt like making their buildings like machines, thinking of usefulness, claiming contemporaneity by using the same materials that the machines did, and having to fake it! Like conjurers, hiding their bricks under stucco, and steel in their concrete to make it go further. The machines were heading fast for *invisible space,* and the architects were too close to the conundrum to see that character, that is, being just like themselves and nothing else, that *character* would hold the day for buildings, and that the machines were dealing in the land, just as they were. At first it was okay. The machines followed human perception for a while; they became clean and dynamic and streamlined, something buildings could be as well, just about. What was the tally ho of the chase? *Pulled into the earth by gravity! Rushing through space at the speed of the turning planet in a hair-raising contretemps with the wind!* It's a cry that would still do.

—— A Short Flight over Public Space ——

When archeologists started looking at the Greek temple pre-
cincts, they could not make out at first what principles of
planning governed the relationships between buildings. They
seemed haphazard and unaligned. It was not until the archeologists unraveled the myths, and how the stories of creation
were thought to inhabit the landscape, that they realized what
was done. The buildings were placed in a landscape vigorous
with meaning. They were set down, not in relation to each
other, but into this—and I hesitate, to savor the phrase—this
charged void. The people who discovered this say it like this,
charg-ed void, in three syllables, to lend it some mystery.

Let's stay with the birds and the planes, and take a ride over
the history of public space. First, the Parthenon. Not planned,
but simply set down, into the *charged void* of the myth-rich
landscape. Next, over the public buildings of Rome, the
round theaters where all the citizens gather together into the
same place, under the same circle of sky. Continue a little
further north, and forward in time, to see Savanarola burning
to death in the Piazza Della Signorina in Florence. The people
gathered round him are waiting for his hair, grown long after
months in jail, to catch light and flare up. Move on again, to
the market square in Delft, full of goods from the Hansiatic
League and stuff carried over the Alps from Persia, and wool
from the chalk plains of England. Next, over the Place de la
Revolution with the guillotine set up and dismembering au-
thority—slicing the capitals off the columns at last, one might
say. That would have been the moment for *ornament is crime*,

when the sansculottes had hammers in their hands! Until at last, we come back to the wasteland, full circle. Wasteland! Why wasteland? It should be called the *liberties,* not the wasteland. It was called *wasteland* by a man who had no eyes to see it, and, well, it is invisible. It's like a *charged void,* full of electromagnetic broadcasts and off-on-on communications, sophistications that only the machines can interpret, but which carry the literature—the drama—to all corners.

This liberties, this new charged void, this public landscape, has almost become a mental phenomenon, made of a consensus of value that changes to accommodate each new opportunity that the machines present. Of course there are many who would disagree with this. The claims for public space are argued like the claims for souls were in the sixteenth century. Have you heard them? The modernist says, "How can you sweep aside two hundred years of progress? With your dreadful old buildings looking like death warmed up!" The classicist replies, "And to you I say, One *thousand* years! One thousand years of civilization. The road I travel on is peopled with the ghosts of venerable men." That one, there—that *ghosts of venerable men* is just what the Jesuit Campion said when he faced his Protestant torturers in the Tower of London in the days of the Armada. I still say the public landscape is more mental than spatial—even the certainties are added to the melting pot. Of course it looks like nothing at all. It looks like garbage—because the consequence of so many conflicting directions is to produce an image of what seems like a garbage dump. There is, however, an option to select—because it's mental. That's why some people like it. They have to see only what they want to see.

There is a coda to this *short history of modern life*. It's another slogan of Le Corbusier's that catches my imagination. *A machine for living in.* There is something about that shuttle and chase plane analogy I used that rings out of tune to me. That's it with analogies, they are the thing that similes and contracted similes—so-called metaphors, which are so much easier to use—allude to; an analogy is a parallel illustration that has to be secure in all its relevant parts. Perhaps I should try another.

I think, like Vitruvius, that architecture includes both buildings and machines, and I think that it includes land-scapes, too. The notion that machines escaped somehow from the tyranny of buildings is more an illustration of what it must have felt like back there in modern times—like being in a plane taking off, hanging on to the arms of the seat with the safety belt tight over your stomach, and staring your own mortality in the face, with your mind blank and your pulse racing.

Machines for living in might refer to something else. Not a machine at all, an analogy itself, in fact. I shall illustrate what I'm thinking of by relating what happened to my friend Jean-Luc in Africa. He's a sculptor now, in Paris, with a commercial life behind him, but when he went to Africa he was selling photocopiers. He was visiting some small town in the trackless, bone-dry desert, as an official guest of the town.

"Heaven knows why the company sent me there," he said, "but they did. *Leave no grain of sand unturned*, I suppose." He always wears English clothes, tweeds and half-skin brogues. Out there in the sand, he must have looked like Leonard Woolley, the archeologist who discovered the hanging gardens of Babylon. Anyway, one day, as an honored guest, he had to sit and watch a punishment take place in the mayor's house. The sun was high and the sky was more than blue, almost turquoise. The reprobate was led into the court-yard, with his hands tied with camel rope. His trousers flapped round his ankles and he had no shoes. "He has insulted the Holy Book," Jean-Luc's hosts kept saying. "He is no better than a jackal. He is as dirty as a dog." The man's family was there, his shamed father, his shamed grandfather, his shamed brothers, and also his little blameless son, for whose honor he had to atone. They stood with their heads bowed in front of a rough stone wall, with the shadow of the arch above falling on their dusty shoulders. Behind the wall their women wailed in misery. On the other side of the court, on a little wooden dais with a fretworked roof, the magistrate and his guests sat on velvet cushions. One of them was Jean-Luc, cross-legged and uncomfortable, a fish way out of water. He crossed his hands over his genitals to shield them from the violent world as the lashes of the whip came smacking down on the man's back. A dreadful wet smack, wet with blood. They passed coffee round.

That night Jean-Luc couldn't sleep, and it took him all of the next day to find words for his protest, but at last he got it out. He chose the mayor's brother, a man just like himself, his own age, his own height, his own education.

"Where I come from," said Jean-Luc, "we did such things five hundred years ago. We burned men alive for blasphemy. Now, we find the practice barbaric, and a man is free to say what he says. Just answer me one question: how long will it take you people to become civilized?"

"Ha!" snorted the other man. That was the sound—snorted. Such contempt in his voice. "Ha! You understand nothing! You are like a child! Our laws belong to God, not us. They will not change in five *thousand* years. You speak of civilization as though you own it—but the truth, my friend, is this," and he said the next bit as though he was in possession of a great truth: "We are more civilized than you will ever be."

Jean-Luc went back to his room and packed his bag, his little, traveling collection of things that had been made in France. By the time he had arrived on the Mediterranean coast, he knew what he thought. It was that this liberty he had—this freedom, this halfway house, *democracy*—it's not a civilization at all. It's not a civilization, it's a mechanism. *A machine for living in.* A way for us all to get along while accommodating the differences between us. The beauty of a machine is that it's neutral, it has no value, except in use. A civilization says who's in charge, who's a slave, sets out what to think in holy books. It makes mountains out of differences. The mechanism, on the other hand, proscribes little, in order to keep a lot possible.

"Yes, you are more civilized than we are," he said, as he stood on the back of the steamer and watched the glittering coast of Africa recede. "That's just your hard luck." *Tant pis pour toi!*

I know that this machine analogy dates back to the revolution. The Americans still talk of a constitution erected with checks and balances against the abuse of power, as though it were built like a steam engine. I think Jean-Luc's machine has more solid-state clusters, fewer moving parts, but it still has the neutrality of the land.

Machine analogies are tricky items. I once came across a man who was trying to build what he called a robot historian. It was armored all over in white ABS plastic and had facial features just like its maker's. He'd even given it a plastic beard.

"What do you call it?" I asked him. He pointed out a circle and two short vertical lines painted on the robot's backpack.

"He's called Off-on-on," he said. He loved his machine. He was like Narcissus, gazing at his own reflection; when the project ran out of funds, he decided to become the robot historian himself, and went about saying what he said the robot would have said. Robot historians view evolution, the whole long process, as the gradual coming into being of intelligent machines.

"It's an evolution whose life force is human desire," he used to say, "and humans are the link between the lower biological forms and the machines." The center piece of the idea is that war is the breeding ground of technology, and so the robot historian sees war as a sort of fertile wonderland.

"Wait one second!" I used to say to him. "War is nothing but confusion, a confusion of conflicting desires."

"Oh, no. War is the coming into clarity of the new machines."

I had to stop and think this out. If Jean-Luc's machine *is* more advanced than the model of 1776, it might well be because of things found out at Pearl Harbor and Khe-San. But that's what I mean when I say the machine analogy is a tricky item. It tends to take on a life of its own. Look at the way we educate our children. The clicking of the grade averages and the ratchet of examinations are almost a torture. I sometimes wonder whether Blake meant schools, not factories, when he wrote about the *dark, Satanic mills*. But I don't think abuses of the analogy disprove the use of it. The enlightenment machine was the sparest of structures, lubricated by self-knowledge, and, in view of the possibilities for revelation experienced daily by a free-thinking person, it's still a valid Utopia.

The Cathedral Church of St. Paul (1710), 29 December 1940. Photograph from Solo Syndication and Literary Agency Limited.

4
THE ART OF THE LAND

A short history is not one that's not long. It's like *short-bread*, made with no yeast. My short history of modern life has no bibliography, no annotation, no corroboration, no listing of primary and secondary sources—it's anecdotal, it has no guarantee of authenticity. It's like literature. It lumps a student throwing his copy of Ruskin in the Seine in 1932 with the battle of Passchendaele in 1917 and the Wright brothers' first flight at Kitty Hawk in 1903 and it says, "Look at that. Modern life." How else can I track the multiple threads I want to bring in if not like this? Corroborated, the thing would be three thousand pages long and as thick as a mystery.

I've suggested that literature carries the complications of modern life like architecture used to carry the civilized life before that; and, I should add, though it risks a complication, like music, in the guise of religion, used to carry the life still further back than that, in the time of crusades and cathedrals. I've attempted to catch the animal—architecture—and put it in a cage—the grand art trilogy—the better to see what it is. Now is the point at which I need to describe it: to look at its nostrils and its anus, to see where it begins and ends. If architecture is, as I say, the art of the land, you would expect it to have edges.

THE ART OF THE LAND

THE FLAMENCO MAGICIAN

There is a great movement now for nothing to have edges. All the arts are striving to be like all the others, painting and dance and opera all *borrowing*, and it's the same with all the sciences, the boundaries between chemistry and physics *dissolving* in the attempt to study the upper atmosphere, and all the professions are becoming like each other, planning and accountancy *merging* to become land management—why should the accountants get that job?—everything borrowing, dissolving, and merging. When I say confusion, I mean *not good*; I'm a fan of clarity, especially of the complex sort. If I want to say *confusion* meaning neither good nor bad, but just mixed up, I use another word: *furor.* So look at the furor that literature is spawning! Literature, the great art of meaning, which connects everything up! Literature, the art of content, has triumphed over architecture, the art of form!

Sometimes, the multitude of voices all speaking their piece at once seems like chaos. The blizzard of information we daily receive sometimes seems blinding, but you don't have to take it all in; *the first thing to do is to be selective.*

The second thing to do is to stand up and be counted. In other words, commit yourself. It's a sort of corollary to

E. M. Forster's great modernist literary slogan "only connect." It means coming to grips with choice. What you have to do, with so much choice, is to choose. And having chosen, to stick with it. Of course the function of a democrat is to vote— that's one part of standing up to be counted. Here's another: I was watching *Measure for Measure* with a friend once, who was at the time thrashing his way through a difficult divorce. In the last sixteen lines of Shakespeare's play, Vincentio, the Duke, resolves everyone's lives for them, condemning one man, raising another, marrying off two couples, and taking the heroine for his wife. My friend leans over to me and yells above the applause, "There's no one like that now! Now, you have to make all your own decisions by yourself!" That's the other part of it, of standing up to be counted. Of course, this responsibility, the responsibility of being equal, is much too hard to bear. Who has time, in the frantic world of work, to think? That's what the aristocracy was invented for. Damn! Let me write like Burke: Democracy is a fragile ship. The whole thing could founder on the rocks of Ethnicity, the new serfdom, where the certainty of belonging overcomes the desire to be free.

———————

Wait a minute—*Literature is content, where architecture is form?*—did I write that? Surely the situation is more complex than that? Surely by now these oldfangled words have been sluiced clean out of the critic's armory. I should have an assistant in a spangled leotard and fishnets and a feather headdress for this bit.

I say to her, "Our act creaks like a biplane."

"And look how lightly they fly," she says. "Think of yourself not as a kamikaze pilot, but as a flamenco dancer. Take up your position before you dance."

That's what all this is, she has just reminded me: not *critical*, but *positional*.

All right. *The flamenco magician*. I take the corner of my waistcoat in my left hand. I rest my right hand on it, holding my fingers straight, as stiff as bones. I point my Cuban-heeled foot, and I say, *There are illusions of form in literature*. The pages of the books, with their margins and footnotes and headings, for one thing, and the structure of letter into word into sentence into paragraph, for the other. Well, it must impress itself onto our senses somehow. The words must have order and form enough to be perceivable, but how many ways there are for them to break into the physical world. Words can be spoken as well as written. They can be coded into morse. They can be transmuted into binary numbers and put on a compact disc and sent down wires. The content stays the same. Here's Hazlitt's essays on my desk. Here's T. S. Eliot's. The books are exactly the same, in structural terms. The *structure* that makes them different in a critical sense is a mental notion. It doesn't *exist*.

Now look at this building. It's a temple, but if it were used as a strip joint, it would still be this shape. The base of the column doesn't *mean* the base of the column—it *is* the base of the column. Look at that concrete bunker over there. It doesn't *mean* the defence of the country—it's part of it. Just as the soldier inside is part of it. That's form. The mess of patriotism running through the soldier's mind, now, his reason for preparing to die for his country—that's content.

What about this cathedral, built on the plan of a cross? Does the cross not mean something?

I flash a look at my assistant to see her reaction: this is a tricky bit. Her face is totally deadpan. "Go on, darling," she hisses between her teeth, "get on with it. It'll be okay."

Okay, to cathedral builders, the cross doesn't *mean* Christianity—it is Christianity. Just like the bread and the wine don't *represent* the flesh and blood of Christ in the mass—they *are* them.

The flamenco magician. I've got a top hat on my head, and I'm hoping my rabbit has not got squashed flat in there.

"Form and content is a ratio," comes a voice from the audience. It's my friend Bob, with his gold tooth flashing in the darkness of faces. I planted him there to lead the applause, but he's leading the heckling instead. "Everything that has a form has a content, and vice versa too. What it is, is a question of ratio."

"Male and female are in ratio," I snap back, "and yet we have men and women!" It's the best I can do. I flip the hat in the air, and the false bottom inside goes *snap* and the rabbit drops into my arms. I pass it to my assistant, who bows—to show off her real bottom, caught in fishnet—and I can move on to the next subject.

——— ARCHITECTURE AND LITERATURE ———

I need to illustrate the art of the land, to describe a machine, a building, and a landscape, to show what I have forged *in this little smithy of my imagination.* First I must take you one more inch to complete the mile of explanation.

I have always been impressed by the emphasis on truth that appeared in the mouths of artists at the turn of the century. Just as the absolute was giving way to the relative—it seems as if the idea of the truth suddenly flared up at the point at which it was about to disappear, like an exploding star. Why should *Truth to Materials* have been such an effective slogan to describe buildings built of brick and then stuccoed, to appear what they called *plastic*? Or built of concrete covered steel with a false steel frame applied to the outside? Or built of reinforced concrete, which hides its tension members as a matter of definition?

This is buildings all over. They are what they are—they're so full of themselves that truth doesn't come into it. There's a Victorian house near me that had to have its plaster quoins remade. When they took them off, you could see that the people who built the house had used cheaper bricks under the quoins, because they would be hidden under the plaster, and yet the quoins are the image of the cornerstones of a stone building, which are emphasized because they are stronger than the rest! *What can you do, when you know so much?*

Truth is like trust. "I swear to tell the truth, the whole and nothing but." Physical corroboration produces evidence, a wholly different thing. Truth and evidence are as different as content and form. Of course, there are many mouths pronouncing on this, but the special nature of the text compared with the spoken word could rest on nothing but the simulation it makes of physical evidence. There is a Borges story, "The Witness," in which he describes the death of the last

Saxon who could remember, firsthand, the old pagan rites. Just as, the blind Borges says, there was a day that extinguished the last eyes to have seen Christ. It is a speculation about the quality of experience set against knowledge. It contains a hint that literature does have its formality, after all. Not in printed works, but in the living tissue of human brains. Only while there is life does literature have a possibility. Meanwhile, set on the stony, implacable ground, we build the experience we call architecture. Some of us, like King Cheops, build it strong enough to withstand atomic blasts.

I have a sort of allegory in which two characters, Architecture and Literature, fight it out for possession of space. Architecture could be played by a guilded hermaphrodite, carrying a spear and wearing Greek sandals. Literature, by one of those balloon-shaped figures from the Bauhaus theater, with a costume of primary colors arranged in a grid, like Mondrian.

Architecture, whose subject space used to be, has been unable either to keep up with the pace set by Literature, by the rapid changing of human minds accomodated in that great fat body, or to acknowledge the significance of machines as a contemporary manifestation of itself, and so decently to retire. As a consequence of that confusion, space, as a certainty, has temporarily disappeared. *There is no there there.* The people mill about the place in confusion, not relishing the hard work of being free—"Oh God!" they cry. "Why do we have to learn so much? We just want someone to love!" They wish that there was some proper space to rely on, and so Literature has stepped into the breach and made a bid for the delineation of space by claiming it as a mental notion.

How can it? How can literature be as steady as rocks, as certain as gravity? Well—it can't. But it is the master of illusion, fact- and fictionwise, so it can seem to be. Literary criticism has been the advance guard of this battle for space. The *text* is posited as a formal entity, the *structure* of the work is taken as a structure in space. The *context* is seen as the terrain for action. It has come to pass that literature is criticized, and consequently written, in spatial terms. You would think that modern fiction had been written by the monks of Whitby thirteen centuries ago, for all its short chapters and cyclical construction and its use of pieces of evidence.

So it's no surprise that when architects turn to literary criticism, in their desire to be inclusive, to borrow, dissolve, and merge, they discover that it fits them to a T. "Hey, this is about us!" they say. "Lookit, it's true! Look at these walls! All the action of architecture happens on the margin!"—and they set about treating nature like a context, like something reciprocal, and they bolt together buildings that look as if they can't be bolted together.

We should remember what happened to Charles the First. "A monarch and his subjects are clean different things," that's what he said. It was the pursuit of antiquity that got him—and for what? Antiquarianism! They had *antique classical* buildings and *antique classical* books and *antique classical* paintings; and his lawyers wanted *antique classical* laws, too, so they could join in. They persuaded him that the life-and-death prerogative of the Roman emperors was preferable to the common law. He swallowed the line and started to become arbitrary. That's why the others had to cut his head off. *A body and its head are clean different things.*

KITTY HAWK

Now for the machines, the buildings, and the landscapes. First, a machine. We need to go to Kitty Hawk, North Carolina, U.S.A. It is a desolate, windy place on that long spit of land that makes an arrowhead out of Cape Hatteras in the atlas—only a mile or two from Roanoke Island, where Walter Raleigh made his first foray of settlement in the New World. The sands of the spit have been lifted by the steady and ever-present wind into a low range of dunes called the Kill Devil Hills. It was from here that the Wright brothers flew their first kites and gliders and eventually, the first powered aeroplane ever seen, the *Wright Flyer*.

There is no such bird as a kitty hawk. There are kites, who soar in the air like huge gulls and inhabit the edges of woods, and there are hawks, smaller, speedier birds who dash after their prey in short, quick flights. No kitty hawks. What's in a name? The brothers said that it was watching the trembling wingtips of the buzzards in Ohio that gave them the idea of warping the wings of their gliders to maintain control. A "buzzard" in America is what a "vulture" is in England. A bird whose head, which is naked of feathers for the ease of slipping it into a sticky carcass, seems too small for its body. Seen flying at a distance, it seems, like a machine, to have no head at all.

What drew the brothers to Kitty Hawk was the loneliness, which meant they might work in peace; the sand, which would cushion the pain of their crash landings; but most of all, it was the wind, which blows in from the sea every day, every single day, at a steady twenty-five knots. The picture of the evolution of the *Wright Flyer* is the determined expression of these two men in this wind. They felt that if only they stood in the wind and stretched their arms in the right way, held their bodies just so, they would be able to fly.

They decided to lie down prone in their gliders, not sit upright with their legs dangling down as Lillienthal had—so as not to be snapped in half in a crash as Lillienthal had been. There is a photograph of Wilbur Wright in No. 2 glider, lying as flat as a biplaned rug on the ground, having just landed. He is still lying there in full flying attitude. His eyes are half closed against the wind, his chin's forward, his body is still cradled in the wooden yoke with which he warped the wings by wriggling his hips—he looks like an allegorical figure, the doomed Icarus. But if you look closely at the photograph, you can see that all around him in the sand are the marks of earlier flights: the footsteps of the running men who launched the glider, the scars of previous landings, some new and urgent, others days old and softened by the consistent wind.

The two brothers built in the summer and flew in the winter, and all through 1900, 1901, and 1902 the sands accumulated these marks of experiment while the gliders flew further and further, watched by three bemused friends from the Kill Devil Hills Coast Guard station. Orville's record photographs are bleak; so few figures in the landscape, all black loden dressed against the cold, and all of them concentrated on the progress of the machines, watching each flight intently for clues to development, always in movement, running alongside, swinging their heads, acting the pilot's movements, anticipating the landings with springing knees in a dance of attendance. Just above all this at fifteen or twenty feet the canvas-covered gliders are like flying roofs over the landscape of sand and men. A dynamic landscape, flattened out to the perfect curve of the launching rail, one where the figures are on it, and not in it or part of it. This is the modern world. No longer the sedate, frock-coated procession of the planets of the neoclassical landscape, nor the jungle of the old flat earth.

The remoteness of Kitty Hawk, and the utter skepticism of the outside world, meant that the first powered flight drew an audience of only five people: the three coastguards, one man, and one boy.

One interested reporter did attend the first powered-circle flight that the *Wright Flyer* made back in Ohio nine months later. He was Amos Root, a bee enthusiast and editor of the bee keeper's journal *Gleanings in Bee Culture*. Studying the mysteries of the beehive had made him farsighted— he mentioned the possibility of a flight over the pole. Even he, however, did not include a flight to the moon, which has now been visited; or the interesting fact that blood and body fluids start to boil above 63,000 feet; and neither did he mention the wind at Kitty Hawk, which is still there, and is the real dynamic of this episode.

I want to describe the secret spaces in St. Paul's, but first, as a preface, consider the Scott Monument in Edinburgh. It is a narrow, blackened, Gothic piece that you can climb up. The staircase is so narrow that you have to hold your breath like a spelunker passing through a narrow tunnel, to make your chest contract. Once up on top, you feel like the whole thing is on the move. The pinnacles whirl against the clouds and your temples thud and your feet stagger. It's all done without a word, or a single moving part. Compared to the hairsplitting, foggy ambiguities of discussion and agreement among humans that constitutes the world of meaning, the proverbs and maxims and fables and morals, the imitations, representations, propositions, and assertions, the pursuit of value—compared to this rich seam, the simple moves of architecture seem dumb. Worldly matters are at stake, here, the matter of the whole wide world. What's dumb about silence? About striding down the ridgeway on top of the curving world? Or huddling together in fear of the great wide fenland sky, us Friends, us Quakers? Those Renaissance rusticated plinths, platforms flat and true on which to build the ideal space, take up the undulations of the ground by being like the rocks themselves, looking like rocks, in courses so heavy they slam into the hillside like nails, with the string course disappearing overhead with every step you take. What's dumb about that?

The central space of St. Paul's Cathedral in London is the transept, above which hovers the inside of the dome and below which lie the bones, minus one forearm set lost at sea, of Horatio Nelson. The outside of the dome can still be seen among this century's towers from the hills around London, a loadstone of quality marking the top of the city's own little hill. Contrary to popular belief, the cathedral does not float—only the old Catholic cathedrals do that. St. Paul's is part of the Renaissance, so it sits, on its plinth, like a palace.

It is not the central space of St. Paul's that is the most important, however, for between the inside dome, all painted with heavenly allegories, and the outside dome, all sheathed in lead, stands a contraption of hair-raising sophistication that hardly anyone sees: a secret device purchased at the expense of gravity that sucks the breath from your body and lifts your feet from the floor.

The constructional complications of masonry domes—feats of engineering that contemporary technology could produce in its sleep, if only the dreams were there—are the very figure of Renaissance ingenuity. There are many double-skinned domes, argued for with passion and built with bravery. I have already mentioned St. Maria del Fiore, in Florence, with its bread and wine shops. At St. Paul's, the astronomer Christopher Wren, inspired by his friend, the devout numerologist Isaac Newton—imagine the conversations between them!—at St. Paul's, Wren stole the chance to use this secret space to challenge the tyranny of the pull toward the center of the Earth.

The secret is held in the brick cone that stands between the inner and outer domes, from which the permanent scaffold for the outer dome is braced and which holds up the nine-hundred-ton lantern, with its ball and cross, at the very top, but which also bears on its inside a phantasm of distorted shapes, designed to be seen from far below on the floor of the transept. These designs appear as a backdrop for the allegories painted on the inside of the inner dome, like heaven itself, swimming in the shafts of light that enter through hidden windows at the top, but this conventional paradise is transformed into a vertiginous nightmare when you are invited by the clerk of works to crawl through a hole in the cone and enter the secret space.

You stand on a catwalk round the very ring of the eye of the inner dome, which lies inverted beneath your feet, with a two-hundred-foot drop before you and all the color and warmth of the cathedral's interior lighting up the underside of your companion's faces. All around you are the weird distortions of the cone's decoration pressing you forward to the drop, while behind and below you the curving top of the inner dome, simple bricks, disappears downward into invisibility like the slide into hell. There is a railing, thank God, around the eye of the inner dome, and it is this you must grasp as your feet leave the floor and you float, weightless and terrified.

The secret spaces of St. Paul's are many. The whispering gallery, the space between the nave and the roof where the inverted saucers of the nave vaults push through the floor like aliens, the crypt itself, where solid and void are held in equal proportion—and they add up to some parallel to the cracking of the invisible mysteries that Newton had accomplished three years before the cathedral was started. His discoveries, made in faith, were the death knell of faith itself, so that even up there in the antigravity device, even while cheating the beast, you can feel the hot breath of his laugh at your back.

This is the sort of thing that buildings can do. As the pyramid at El-Giza stands for all time, as Chartres marks the spot, as the square in Sienna is the repository for everything in the city, as the cenotaph at Tiepval brings you to your knees. Dumb, compromised, mundane maybe; but this is the sort of thing that buildings can do. Mundane sounds like *humdrum*, but it means *of the world*; worldly. Both the steady progress of the Wright brothers and the echoing achievements of Wren and Newton could be described as mundane, of the world. Here's another one: Compromise sounds weak, but it means *bind*—as in promise—*together*. It represents the end of the argument, the conclusion. In physical terms it means the fitting together of the parts.

I don't want to let St. Paul's go by without adding this item I came across in Banister Fletcher's *History of Architecture*. It was published at the turn of the century, when baroque was still considered *despicable;* and it concerns the screen wall of the cathedral, which adds an apparent second story to the building. Sir Banister notes that considerable criticism has been directed against this screen wall, *which is said to be a sham:* he suggests that these objections might be removed *if the wall were pierced with openings to show the flying buttresses behind.* He's even done a little drawing of the subject. Let's make sure the dome's not going to fall first, hey?

So now for landscapes. What are landscapes? I have two examples, one sentimental, the other dispassionate, something to bring us back full circle to the machine. And I have dry stone walls. I met a farmer in the hills of Yorkshire who told me about dry stone walls. He was a solitary man. He had two of those half-wild sheep collies with him, who boiled round our feet the whole time we were talking, me in my Berghaus polar-plus jacket and my Craghopper britches and my Scarpa Attack fell walkers with a compass and a pair of binoculars round my neck, and he in his waistcoat and trousers and army boots and a silver fob watch in his pocket, which he set by the movement of the sun in the sky. It was autumn, and he was out rounding up his half-wild sheep for *tupping*—that is, for mating. Tup is the name they have up there for the rams—and also, incidentally, for the massive iron heads of the old steam hammers. It makes you think that that's what they thought sex was like, in nineteenth-century Rochdale—the action of a steam hammer!

"You don't plan a dry stone wall," this man said to me. "You don't look forward to it, you don't anticipate it. You just build it."

"Straight up the hills," I said, squinting into the sun. These walls, they don't follow contours, or wiggle round outcrops, they go straight up the hills, like Roman soldiers on the march.

"That's because you never stand back when you're building a dry stone wall. You always have your nose up close to what you're doing."

"Like a mountain sheep," I suggested.

"Like everything. Dog sniffing, ram tupping." He winked at me and the little veins in his cheeks filled with blood and made him blush. "No, what you do is do it step by step," he went on. "There are stones all over the field. Look around you—there they are, all over." I looked, and yes, everywhere in the limestone country the moors are studded with stones—most of them a good size for building with, about twelve inches across and weighing, what? Fourteen pounds?

"You collect up all the stones and get them in a big pile where the wall's going to be. Now, that's the last time you're going to look at that pile of stones. What you do is reach behind you, pick the first stone that comes to hand, and place it on the ground. Keep doing that. Reach behind you, pick a stone and, whatever shape or size it is, you place it in the wall. Nice and snug, nice and tight. Whatever way it fits in best. No knocking off the edges, see? No bedding it in mortar. Just stones from the field all resting together. That's a dry stone wall." He looked so addled with wisdom I thought my heart would break. I went on my way and the great fells stood like they always had, like timelessness. They swooped around me like a symphony. Well, why not?

My first landscape is the Vale of the White Horse. The White Horse is an ancient figure cut into the chalk hills of Lambourn below one of the Iron Age castles that are situated on the Ridgeway. The figure dances on the horizon like the horizon itself. It might not be a horse at all; it might be a dragon, no one knows, but its shape is long and fluid, like the shape of the chalk hills themselves. It is a complete work of architecture made with one action, the removal of the turf. The turf on the chalk uplands is only six inches thick, and underneath is the cream white rock. It shows up against the green grass even better than black on white.

The views up there are enormous. On one side is the steep flank of the hill, as close as the flank of a pack animal to its driver, and on the other is a clear view for fifty miles across the vale of Oxford. Ahead of you is the horse. You walk toward it watching its shape undulate with the change in perspective. It lies on the hill in front of you just beneath the sky. The children think it must be the shape of the dragon that St. George slew, stretched out dead on its side. When you reach it, and stand in it, it is so precisely located among the folds of the grass that it becomes a miniature of the huge landscape around you, and you feel like a giant, standing on top of the world. It is the perception of the Ridgeway journey made tangible, like a thought spoken.

My second landscape involves a visit to the planetarium. You can't see it from down here on earth.

The names of the stars, like the names of the birds and the bees, are held in scholarly minds in Latin. The classification of the fauna and flora is precise; all toads are *Bufo*, for example, but only the common toad is *Bufo Bufo*. The system was established by Linneaus in the eighteenth century, when to be modern was, unlike us, to be antique at the same time as rational; hence the Latin. The naming of the stars, on the other hand, is not the work of this organized age. It follows an ancient pictorial system of a quite different sort of science whose source is the myths of Greece and Rome, of Hercules, Perseus, and Orion. The planetarium's narrator can tell you about it: "On the edge of the *Heavenly Sea* rests the great ship *Argo*, made up of four constellations and with a fifth, *Columba*, to one side. Columba the dove, that is, whom the Argonauts followed, through the clashing rocks and into the Black Sea."

This enormous convention of forgotten names and stories is one thing. Their apparent formation may one day be another; in outer space, the pictures will dissolve like a dew as the earthbound perspective that maintains them disappears. In the blackness space travelers might go mad, like Hamlet teasing Polonius about the shape of the clouds.

These thoughts were redeployed by the Apollo astronauts who visited the moon and gave it their bewildered, undivided, and scientific attention. They were terrified by the isolation but trained in self-control and the antimadness value of sentimentality. When these twelve air force pilots got in among the craters and rocks that couldn't be seen from the earth and started the job of naming them, they forgot about the *Mare Tranquillitatis* of distant contemplation and went instead for home and immediacy: Split Rock, Weird Rock, Smoky Mountain, Spook Crater, Buster Crater, and— perhaps one of them came from Florida—*'Gator Crater*. Their excursions to the moon left behind a fine collection of rubbish, all the more endearing for the fact that one can make a complete inventory of human rubbish for the whole planet: around fifty pieces in all. What would be a giant task for the earth is a small job on the moon. Survey vehicles, hand carts, cameras, all of it glittering silver, black, orange, and gold in the bright sunlight and destined to stay that way for thousands of years, together with the footprints of the twelve men.

The mystery of the moon may have gone, but it has been replaced by clarity. Events that on earth would have been eroded to nothing by the wind and the rain stand out as features on the arid moon landscape. Even the track of a boulder rolling down a hill, disturbed by some ancient land settlement, is still there today and will remain sharp and clear forever. And in this deathly quiet, everlasting, airless terrain the leftovers of human activity stand out as bright as a city, as moving as a cathedral floating over its country town, but looking like the aftermath of a picnic.

***Phoebus Apollo* (The Pantheon, Rome, 124).** Photograph by John Mosse/The Architectural Association Slide Library.

INTERLUDE

The forecast was for a red moon. The shadow thrown by the earth in an eclipse of the moon is not all black: the sunset glows red at the edge of the penumbra, and so from some parts of the earth, the moon glows with it. It's not quite a once-in-a-lifetime event like Halley's comet, but it's a rare enough thing to be worth seeking out, and so I had traveled down to Ditchling to see it with Steve and Sally and Jean-Luc and Conrad. We climbed the high hill there, taking it in turns to wheel the old man's chair, and up on the top we found a host of other people gathered. A small crowd out of doors at night, watching the sky—it seemed ancient. It seemed like being in on the beginnings of Stonehenge. We had the feeling, we gave voice to it, that this is how architecture got started in the past. There was a beautiful quiet darkness while everybody waited for the moonrise. A perfect moment to tell stories.

Sally's story was about the moon, and about the way a building wants to be—about Lou Kahn, the grand old man of the east, who could hypnotize anyone with that "building wants to be" kind of talk, taking two of his bemused clients to the plot they had bought for their house in the old Indian country above Philadelphia. It was three o'clock on a dark night, the three of them all wrapped up in blankets against the chill like Sitting Bull, and Kahn made them kneel down in the bracken while the sun came up, and he described in a quiet voice what it would be like in the *den* at *dawn* with the riven slate floor he was going to use as black as ink in the morning light. . . . *The building wants to be.*

The sky got darker and darker as we sat there, and Jean-Luc described the Tenebrae service in Holy Week, where all the lights of the church are extinguished one by one, as the psalms are sung. It commemorates the darkness supposed to have come over the earth at the time of the crucifixion. The eclipse of Christ's death is a metaphor, said Jean-Luc, so inside the tiny world of the church building they dramatize it, and make it seem real.

It was all too gentle—too cosy and mystical—for Steve. He always has been one for this "at Agincourt they built ramparts out of the dead bodies of French soldiers" sort of stuff. He calls it *Human Stones.* Violence is an intrinsic part of making space, his argument goes. He started to tell us another part of his Cinderella routine, about the Grimm brothers' version of the story—*Ashiepattle*—about a piece at the end that the sanitizing Perrault has hidden from us. Prince Charming comes in with the tiny slipper on a cushion, looking for Cinderella's tiny foot. First, one of the vain sisters tries it on, and it's only when they are halfway back to the castle, the sister proudly riding the prince's horse, that he notices blood oozing from the slipper where she has cut her toes off to make it fit.

Steve raised his fist. "The only constant is change!" he said, and we all laughed at him. What else should you do with an oxymoron? Just at that moment a shooting star flashed across the sky and Jean-Luc saw it first and lifted his arms and said, "Yes! I have luck now!" This hard-headed, liberal Frenchman believed in luck. He raised his arms out with his fingers in a V in the peace-love-victory sign, then pressed his hands together across his heart, then raised them to his lips and kissed them, and stretched out his arms again, his fingers quivering in a gesture of yearning, toward the vanished star.

"Holy cow," said Sally. "You look like you're taking a bow at the opera!" And Jean-Luc was, indeed, imitating a Spanish tenor's sequence of thanks for applause that he had witnessed one night at La Scala. Peace, from my heart, it means, with my love, to you all.

I don't know why, perhaps it was the Disney-moon-dust character of the thing, but my mind flashed back to a scene in the woods up above Dumfries. I had been walking with my young son when we came across a dead badger. It had been dead for quite a while, and it was lying on its back with its skin all stretched and tanned a beautiful chestnut maroon by the weather. All its hair had gone, except for a few spare brushes on its whip of a tail, and its lips were shriveled up into a snarl under its empty eye sockets. What huge yellow teeth it had! John picked up a stone and hurled it at the corpse, and it went straight through the skin like a bullet, and this dreadful slimy mass oozed out of the hole. A dreadful smell came out along with it, and all of a sudden the whole place was filled with the smell of rotten flesh, and we ran away from it as though the little ghoul had reared up and spat at us. There you are, Steve, I thought. You could make a building out of that.

A voice at my side interrupted my thoughts. "Well, you old fucker," it said, "still solvent after all these years?" I turned round to see Terry. *Terry the builder*, the one who had built those tower blocks that collapsed, built them as casually as he might have cooked his breakfast. I still hadn't forgiven him for dumping me in it.

"You're out of jail already!" I said.

"I got out yesterday," he said. "I haven't seen the moon for two bloody years, that's why I'm here."

I lit a match, like an explorer who finds himself cut off by a rock fall in some ancient temple, and took a close look at him.

"You've changed," I said, as the flame died down. Even in the dark I could see that his hair problem had disappeared, and he was covered in black curls.

"I've spent my time wisely," he said. "I'll never forgive them for banging me up, but I didn't waste the time. I'm going into the restoration business."

"But Terry," I said, "you don't know anything about anything!"

"I do—I've been studying. Studying buildings. Go on—ask me something."

"Ask you what?"

"Ask me something about cathedrals."

Ah, bloody cathedrals, is it. They've been lurking around this whole enterprise like wolves on the prowl. They 'seem to be the whole answer to every question I ever asked about architecture, and I can't put my finger on it. And here's this jailbird, flown in to tell me all about it. So I said, "How can I stop thinking about them?"

He was as quick as a fish. "Cathedrals aren't buildings at all. They're solid prayers."

"*What?* Not buildings?"

"That's right. Corb said they were built drama, which I personally think is a little off target." *Corb?* This was definitely not the Terry I used to know. "Corb had to get the cathedrals off his back, as well. They don't seem to fit into theories of what architecture is, because they're not architecture. Think about it: everything was prayer back then, everything that was written, all the battles that were fought—work, war, politics—all prayer; why not buildings?"

It was still night, we were still on top of the hill, we had still come to see the red moon. What is all this? The others had gathered round to see what we were talking about.

"I've heard of baroque buildings being called *frozen music,*" Sally put in. She didn't sound too sure what this had to do with it.

"No, no, no," said Terry, "if anything, that's music being fluid buildings."

"The Jesuits invented baroque to manifest the spiritual exercises, didn't they?" I said, just trying to keep my end up. It felt like poking a stick into a hole to see if there was a rattlesnake down there. Terry didn't miss a beat.

"In the beginning of it, maybe, where they covered the surfaces with mystery—but that frozen music stuff, that's something else, that's fashion."

He took a packet of biscuits out of his pocket and started putting them in his mouth, one after another. Then he remembered he was no longer in prison. "Cookie?" he said, pointing the packet at me.

"No thanks," I said, "but clear something else up for us. What's the difference between sculpture and architecture?"

It was like pressing buttons—he didn't seem to reflect at all before opening his mouth. Is *this* what artificial intelligence will be like? "Sculpture is the same thing as architecture, but carried on in a solitary form," he said, with his mouth full of crumbs. "Like poetry and music. You know that thing where poetry is not heard, but overheard? It separates lyric poetry out from literature and puts it in with music. It forces its audience to be solitary. That's what sculpture does to space. Wraps it up and gives it to you, alone."

Another *cookie* went into his mouth and he looked so complacent I was sure that Steve was getting ready to thump him—but then Jean-Luc joined in with something that shut us all up. And what did Jean-Luc think about the similarity between sculpture and architecture?

"In the Place de la Concorde in Paris," said Jean-Luc, "there is erected the obelisk taken from the banks of the Nile. The obelisk is cut from the living rock, and carries in hieroglyph a description of the glory of Ramses. The distance from the plinth of the obelisk to the edge of the pavement is thirty meters. This is precisely the distance at which a human voice talking becomes inaudible."

The moon was up now, but it still looked as silver as a spoon. The top of the hill was full of people now, and someone had set up a huge ostentatious telescope, one of those where you sit with your back toward your subject and look at it through a prism. The rest of us were gazing up at the sky, and from up there on the hill we were on we could see the lights of towns, as well, spread out across the vale for thirty miles. Then, as we waited and watched, a coppery glow came over the moon—just as they said it would. The very faintest redness stole across its face. I stood and exulted at this evidence of the conclusive world—the moving shadow of the earth cast across another planet—and it wasn't until we were on our way down the hill again that we all started to argue about what it was, exactly, that we all had seen.

USS Birmingham (SSN-695) in a trial high speed ascent (1978). Official U.S. Navy photograph by Newport News Shipbuilding Co.

5
WHAT IS NEXT?

The excitement of these things—landscapes, buildings, machines—is the excitement of others, the others who built them. To understand the devotion of the masons of Chartres, to understand the ambitions of the Wright brothers, the gall of Newton and Wren, the laissez-faire of the astronauts, is to open up the closed box of conclusive meaning, which otherwise remains the thing which is *beyond words*. Beyond words, not because it is the mysterious working of the spirit, but because the subject itself—architecture—is not literature. To talk and write there must be people, somewhere, and the way to talk and write about landed things is to make sure you don't confuse the intentions with the results—and don't take the explanations given by the progenitors as the whole story.

It is one thing to write about what has happened, but if I look at my list of books on architecture, I find them packed with detail on what could happen next. Vitruvius offered practical advice, Palladio made an advertisement for his buildings, Chambers offered patterns to copy. Ruskin made a declaration for the one and only way of Christian architecture, and Le Corbusier propagandized the modern age like a dictator. Who else is there? Venturi, perhaps? He cataloged a mass of architectural inventions, all good useful stuff. Who is it whom I've left out? *Alberti*, of course, the most ambitious, who attempted to make a set of principles by which good architecture might prevail.

This is great company. I am prostrate before their greatness. I should bathe my face in ashes before even writing their names. Still, this is the democratic age, and surely the fleas may go into seminar with the dogs. I persuade them to read my book: "If that's what architecture is," they growl, "what does it look like?" Because, of course, in those books I listed, there it all is, fully described.

WHAT IS NEXT?

──────────────── The Kilt ────────────────

Throughout *What Is Architecture?* I have been repeatedly stating the generality of the human desire to shape the land to suit itself, and then retreating from it into specific examples. So I'll do it again. I'll describe some prospects for architecture as they appear to me, lit up by what I've said so far, and arranged as a sort of appendix to the rest of what I've written. Not in so much detail as to show the walls and columns and moldings and ornament, you understand, but at least some strategies and at least the start of some tactics, too.

"What is architecture?" is not the same question as "What should architecture be?" None of what I have written has been organized to indicate a course for architecture to take. Indeed, one of the implications of it all is that what we are able to theorize as space now—not only the gorgeous pieces, but also the metered relationships, the collections of emphasis, the garbage dumps—is as likely to be accidental as intentional. All of it is architecture, all the good buildings and the bad together, the striven-for landscapes with the ones that appear as a result of some other activity; the machines of war with those of peace. There is one condition to it all, the land; and one motivation, human desire.

Not everything is equally possible all the time. Human desire is the spring of art, and it changes through time; it depends on circumstance. Oratory, the art of persuading others, is a sort of primal technology. It would, as Buckminster Fuller pointed out, be possible to produce all the world's electricity with giant hydroelectric energy systems circling the globe just south of the arctic circle—but do any of us want that enough to thrash through the mountains of politics in the way?

Another thing—skills can be lost as well as acquired. There is a story that fragments of each of the seven wonders of the world were once collected together and mixed with sand and cement into a little concrete block by a Roman traveler who forsaw the ravages of the coming age. It ended up in the hands of Michael Psellus, secretary to the Byzantine kings. He used it as a paperweight, and one day he lost it: it was gone forever. Even knowing the enormous amount that we do, some things are beyond us. The pyramids of El-Giza, the cathedrals of the northern plain, the pleasure dome of Kublai Khan. Even the homely Jacobean palaces of England are beyond us. So what is within us?

First of all, we may not make good tombs, but we can make good machines. Good here means good in their own terms, not morally good: there are now technologies, mostly among the highfalutin exotica of weapons research, that promise ways of altering space as profoundly as the first hut meta-phorized the ancient forest into the first civilization. I want to describe some of those.

Also, there is the phenomenon of the machine building, the "shed-off-the-peg," as the brothers Grimm would have called it. Inside the shed is equipment worth ten times as much as the shed itself. It is the negative image of that Jacobean palace, where almost all the investment is in the fabric of the building. With all that expensive stuff on the loose inside, what is it that goes on the outside?

Second, I want to say three things about landscapes. One is that every piece of architecture has to be secured in a land-scape. Especially if there is a new direction—there must be a landscape strategy that positions it. Oppositional theories, which, being all intention, are essentially literary, are not good enough. They will sound exciting—temperatures will rise—but they will not guarantee quality.

Then there is time. Perception of the land is not like revelation, it comes about slowly. When it arrives, it is as sure as the day is, but there's a long dawn to sit through first. Have we got the patience?

The third thing I want to say about landscape is that the remaining empty wilderness land, which comforts the city by its mere existence, was once the terrifying wilderness the city walls were built to overcome in the first place. Is it not now time to welcome it inside?

So I shall describe some high technologies and some aspects of landscape; what shall I do about buildings? This *desire* I have been mentioning, this desire to reshape the physical world to fit the humans. I think that in the end this is the way that all good architecture has appeared, as a response to desire, the more urgent the better. It is lodged in our genes for survival, but it has gone further than that. It is general, in the way it can be compared with the desire to be understood, or the desire to know the future—but since it is spatially bound, it has a genius for singularity. Right through the history of human beings, *lodged in the cracks of the great stones of events,* are anecdotes of people whose lives have reached such a critical state that buildings have appeared round them, just like that, like magic. They are tiny buildings, most of them, no more than one room thick: I want to describe a few of those.

Before I do all this, just let me mention the kilt. The original garment is a twelve-foot by six-foot plaid that can be worn around the waist and thrown over the shoulder, secured by belt and broach, during the day. At night the clansman lays the rectangle out on the ground, lies down on it naked, and wraps it round himself to sleep in. So what is architecture?

MACHINES

Camouflage

On the plains of northern France in 1917, all the armies participating in the conflict—American, French, British, German—had a different camouflage. Though they were fighting over the same terrain, using the same tactics in the same corners of the same fields, their camouflages had different shapes and colors to them. I suppose there are camouflage designers—what a job!—and everyone's eyes are different, slightly. Or perhaps camouflage is the ultimate committee decision—"hands up all you who can still see this!"

In wartime the mentality of camouflage gets everywhere. If you had to color code four things, what colors would you choose? Red, blue, yellow, and green? In 1943 the French Resistance, the *Maquis*, color coded their targets. Railway installations, fuel dumps, power stations, and roads—a sophisticated infrastructural bunch, they must have been—and the colors they chose were maroon, khaki, brown, and black.

I am reminded here of something Sally once said to me. "Camouflage takes the ends and edges of a thing and regrades it into the background just like the schooling on a little boy," she said. She's not the only one who dislikes the way we educate our little ones, but what can we do? Education is the answer to everything. It's the liberal's only weapon.

"What's *city* camouflage, then?" I asked her. She had no doubts. She said it was the terrorists who shop in chain stores for clothes, just like everyone else, the better to merge into the crowd.

The attraction of camouflage in peacetime lies in the mediation it makes between human perception and the land. There is a delinquent question which goes, How do I know when I see red that you see the same thing? Delinquent, I say, because it's a confusion, a confusion between perception and meaning. The name matters and the fact of red matters, but they don't matter in the same way. It goes on the same shelf, this confusion, as Zeno's paradox a confusion between space and time—and the question of the chicken and the egg—a confusion of the general with the particular. Confusions have some sort of answer in camouflage, not because it's ambiguous, but because it's illusory. If you think of style, now, as a camouflage instead of an expression, what a difference that makes: style is put on the carcass of the building not so much to proclaim its meaning as to obscure the neutrality of the entity underneath.

There used to be a bunch of aesthetic guerillas based at Maidenhead, you could call them a sort of *hippy Maquis,* whose mission was to put bombs in ugly and presumptuous buildings, to disfigure them. They never had access to the sort of ordnance required to do the job properly, and so they only managed to do superficial damage—but what wonderful damage it was! It was like blowing off the face of a statue— those claddings and canopies, those huge sheets of glass; the five or six inches of depth that decides whether a building is this style or that can be knocked clean off, leaving the neutral entity in plain view.

Camouflage used to be like the spots on a leopard, but now it has changed. It used to be a question of painting on the shapes and breaking up outlines and using colors to make things seem to disappear. Or, like the leopard's pale underbelly, which diminishes the rounding effect of the shadow, to use optical illusions to confuse estimates of range. Now that machines do the work of spotting and targeting, the camouflage has changed to deal with sensors instead of eyes.

Those stealth bombers are not painted black to evoke menace, or to disappear into the night: this is *ablative black*. The paint is full of ferrite particles that absorb radar energy and make the machines harder for the other side's radar to see.

It is difficult to see how character survives in such an environment. Here's an example: the big black submarines that cruise on station under the Atlantic Ocean are invisible, and apparently anonymous. But throughout the life of the machine, the hull picks up dents and scratches exclusive to itself, and consequently the sonar signature of each machine is slightly different. It acquires character through use.

The difference between the old sensual camouflages and the new is that what you see is not what matters, but what matters makes a difference to what you see. As a tactical proposition, that sounds like the modernist maxim of *expression of purpose*. What the modernists perceived about the way machines change space was important, despite their hopeless fantasies of consensus. Machine-made space is not planned, it's a consequence. When you put that together with the idea of style as a camouflage—the cover a neutral entity is given to give it an illusory meaning—you see how interesting camouflaged buildings could become.

The Second Echelon

The old B-52 bombers, designed to unload iron bombs from stratospheric heights, have been pressed into a low-level delivery role for cruise missiles. To handle the stresses of fast, low-level flight, actuators have been fitted to their hulls that press against the structure to keep it firm at critical moments in the headlong rush. Flexing their muscles like iron pumpers on their way to a real fight. This temporary stability is traded for the advantage of not having to carry redundant structure.

HESH is an antitank shell that doesn't explode or penetrate, but which slams against the outside of the tank with such a thud that the inside shatters into shrapnel all over the occupants. *Doing one thing to effect another.*

Perhaps this is the place for a small apology. The frontier technologies I am describing are all to do with killing people. It's because the military appeal "It's life or death!" attracts the most research money: read Vitruvius. There is confusion, also: military technologies are so advanced that they sometimes have an abstract air to them, like the attempts to predict the unpredictable fall of V2 rockets on London in 1944, and abstraction is as open to contamination by narratives as an agar dish in a high school laboratory is to bacteria.

This apology, however, is not about confusion, it's about *knowing what your business is.* These machines can't be talked about without straying out of the matters of the land into moral ground. If we are dealing with other people, there must be a moral question. In this case, Why are we killing them? Why can't we settle it by talking? War itself is the confusion of ideas and reality—but no more mixed up, in the end, than the human mind when it yearns to leave the limitations of its body.

As the soldiers say, it's not guns that kill people, it's people—and I still have more to say about the guns.

To get back to the *second echelon*, doing one thing to effect another: it can be seen in the way character transcends usefulness. Not so much in early machines, which wear their results openly, with their straining wings and their grand smokestacks and their wheel spokes dancing backward in the cine projector gate. Now we know more about the way it's done. There is a second layer of activity in machine design, where the designer is close up to the board, thinking of nothing but the payoff, taking it from where the last one left off, making the best of a bad job sometimes, doing one thing in order to achieve another.

This is what I call the *second echelon*. In any structure there will be enough slack for someone to exploit the interstices. In the natural world, the parasites, the viruses and cuckoo chicks, do it. It might take great courage, but in the tightly organized urban crust of the civilized world we live in now, for example, there will always be room for nomads.

Nap of the Earth

Nap of the earth is the name given to the techniques of exploiting the battlefield. It is the oldest thing, the fundamental skill that all great generals have held in one hand, while holding decisiveness in the other. The new name helps tacticians to extend the processes of guerilla warfare to higher levels of firepower, though it still means hiding behind rocks like cowboys and crossing the forest without snapping twigs, like indians. Helicopters with names like *Iriquois* and *Apache* have gunsights on masts, so they can hover behind trees. The terrain-following radar in the nose of the tactical strike fighter senses the hills and dales and adjusts the height of the plane automatically, keeping it fast and low while the pilot and the navigator stay glued to the complications of sorting friend from foe. But never mind the machines. This is *nap of the earth*. More to do with the way you do things than what you do. *Greener?* Since I'm using a military analogy I should say *olive-drabber*—but in this case, the cliché fits. Nap of the earth implies a close fit between the architecture and the ground it occupies. Not a "contextual" fit with the other buildings; nor a "programmatic fit," with its users; but a fit in the vernacular sense. Opportunistic, energy efficient, buildable, and wise.

Aegis

Camouflage, the figure; second echelon, the technique; nap of the earth, the process; and lastly now, Aegis—the "charged void," the "abstract presence."

The USS *Ticonderoga* is a guided missile cruiser, but it looks just like a container ship painted battleship gray. When it sails with the U.S. Navy's sixth fleet in the Mediterranean, it is not there for its guns or its speed: it is a huge floating radar transmitter. It surrounds the other ships in the fleet with an electronic security blanket as wide as the ocean, as deep as the sea bed, and as high as the sky. The sea and air for eighty miles around become alive, like the hairs on a stinging nettle, a *charged void* into which you enter at your peril. All the ships, submarines, aeroplanes, torpedoes, missiles, and bombs that penetrate this charged void are instantly and automatically plotted, and if necessary, destroyed. They call this system *Aegis*.

Aegis is not some baroque Pentagon acronym. It is a proper name, with an ancient Greek history. Zeus, king of the gods, whose terrible power was both triggered and tempered by his rapacious ambition, had a shield called Aegis.

This much the Pentagon knows. The name was also given to the goatskin-covered breastplate worn by Athene—first the goddess of civilization, then the goddess of war—and into the skin was woven the names of the four qualities of victory: fear, strife, defense, assault. It sounds just like the motto of a battalion of the U.S. Marines. The space that surrounds us is radioactive as a phenomenon of its natural state, and perhaps we have some sixth sense that perceives it. Contemporary life surrounds us in addition with an interpretable radiation, with domestic and commercial signals as well as military ones. Our receiving machines, our radios and televisions, extend our senses into an invisible, intangible arena. The thrust of research has sought out this invisible space and trapped the ether in silicon chips. We are out of the realms of human perception here, but we are still within the land—we shall have to be strapped into machines to live the life promised. Or perhaps we could set them to automatic and let them do all the work, and wander round in togas with flowers in our hair, wanting for nothing, being learned and promiscuous.

Well! There's no picture of the future that's not an allegory of the present. If you want to know what it's really like, you'll have to wait until we get there.

Zeppelin Tech

Compared to all that military stuff, what's called high tech in building today is really zeppelin tech, all aluminum and lightweight frames and modular construction and close tolerances. That's one thing.

Another is that if NATO had had a different strategic posture from that of a crab—defensive in an offensive shell, like that poor king crab in the zoo, who spends all day stock still under his artificial lightbulb sun, with his huge claws covering his eyes, ready for anything: if it had been something else, Napoleonic, say, or Alexandrian, the technical spinoff might have been different. Perhaps we might have been buying personal sets of wings to fly around with instead of personal computers.

Now the new machines are being encouraged to think for themselves—they call it *artificial intelligence*. Some people say that their thoughts will be primitive, that they will react like Cro-Magnons, and that their first response will be to enslave us—mistaking us for chimpanzees. If we leave all the development of artificial intelligence to the military, as Manuel De Landa—the man who invented the robot historian—warns us, that may indeed be so. But if their thoughts take up where ours left off, it might mean that we could be freed into being primitive ourselves—and rebuilding the seven wonders of the world—while the machines get on with being smart.

———————————— LANDSCAPES ————————————

Strategy

The theory of action whose levels are given the names strategy, tactics, and operations comes down to us from ancient times. For those who like their theories foursquare, you add logistics.

Strategy is the motivation, the overview. Tactics is the positioning of parts ready for the implementation of the strategy. Operations is the carrying through. Yes, the theory has a military origin—the *Strategus* was the office of the General—but it stands as an analysis of action and is useful in any situation where intention and material have to be combined.

My trilogy of landscapes, buildings, and machines does not escape the military theory's influence. I think that the center of formal activity is tactics, the business of putting things into position, and it seems to me that this is what buildings correspond to. This centrality goes some way toward explaining the synonymity that has arisen between the words *architecture* and *building*. If I carry on in this way, I find that machines are operational, and that landscapes are strategic, and that architects do all of them.

Whenever I've touched on landscape before, it's been as if my legs have gone weak, and I've been like a Mohican, down on my knees, glorying at the wonder of the rising sun. When I mentioned the White Horse earlier, I said that architecture as landscape is a perception made tangible. Now I am saying that it is a prerequisite of architectural action to have a landscape strategy to frame it. There it is, in Philadelphia—the gridded landscape of liberal rationalism. There it is, in Antipater's seven wonders of the world—the forested, flat earth studded with the first civilizations' feats of building. There it is, in the gardens of the eighteenth century, the ruins of antiquity set in a landscape of stories, a themed landscape.

The detached understanding of the land we build to now is not as simple to describe as those three, but there must be some equivalent way to describe it. Here's one version. When you next walk through the streets of the city and comprehend its cacophonic turbulence, think about it—the crashing canyons of white noise reflected off those mirrored glass towers is the noise of a huge economic perception, a perception of the land turned to account. When you next drive down the highway on a burning hot summer's day, you'll see it. It's a landscape of infrastructure—roads and power lines—and wealth exchangers—villages and cities—all set in a vast agricultural machine. It is a utilitarian theory of landscape of huge finality, compared to which that of the seven wonders of the world, let alone the *perception made tangible,* is as delicate as the nostrils of a horse.

The happy wasteland of liberated souls that I tried to evoke in my short history of modern life is another description of the same landscape. What seems like chaos, the history says, is just the side effect of enthusiasm and busy people. Never mind the rubbish, it says, we are still in the middle of an experiment here; eventually things will become clearer and we can start to demolish the bad and leave the good. In the background as I say this, there is the unmistakable sound of another voice, which knows exactly what it thinks—"and we will live in the glorious emptiness of the flat earth," it says. Let us hope that the flat earth, like the round, can also be free.

What can landscape architects do? While the machines proliferate all over the place, and the buildings try to be one damn thing after another, what can they do? They can dress the space left in between buildings. They can ameliorate the effects of roadworks. Someone has to do it. They can work as environmental auditors. They can work as conservationists, too, reclaiming land spoiled by industry. They can manage the national wilderness parks with a grip so tight it turns their knuckles white, and, of course, they can design theme parks.

Now *theme* is an odd word. It means a subject, in literature, a base melody, in music. How does it belong in architecture? Its etymology suggests a sort of spatial proposition, a thing laid down for consideration. I think of it as a posture within a strategy.

What we know as *theme parks* use the word in a literary sense. There, it is a sort of background story that you have to know first. In such places, where the land is the matter, *park* is the important part of theme park, not *theme*. Take the rational-naturalist landscape at Stowe, for example, where the theme is *Whigs*, or that at Stourhead, where the theme is *Aeneas*, and look at the park—the trees and the hills and the lakes of them—instead. It works with EPCOT, too. When I see a geodesic, I think of the air force, not Mickey Mouse.

But if *theme* is a subject in literature and a base melody in music, there is something it is in the landscape, too. In my phrase *a perception made tangible*, it's the perception: it's the jelly between the senses and the extra human world— it's the human version of the landscape. It is as volatile as jet fuel, this thing. It has a tendency to become literature without your even noticing what's happened, and to keep it *landed* sometimes takes a heroic effort.

This is where the landscape architects might be closest to fulfilling their strategic role, in this matter of the theme, after years of sapping in the front line. After years of making good after buildings and setting up machines and swinging along on the coattails of the engineers. Any new direction in architecture has to be secured in a landscape strategy. The classical revival is a case in point. At the moment, the classicists are busy patching up the city, redressing the fronts and filling in all those gaps left by the modernist dream of towers in green fields. They can't go on like this. Sooner or later they will have to solve the problem of what the city is, because it's not what it was in Alberti's time. They could take a lesson from the master. Alberti knew what change was—he wasn't restating Vitruvius, he was transforming it, and there needs to be another transformation of the landscape before the classical revival can be as good as they say it is. I hope that someone's working on it: it would make a lot of people happy.

Time

One of the puzzles of the stone circle at Stonehenge is a cluster of about forty post holes situated in the northeastern gap of the perimeter ditch. The holes are arranged in six rows, concentric with the stone circle, and radiating from the center as a grid. Current speculation is that the holes are a record of midwinter moon risings as seen from the center of the circle. On midwinter's day, in the late afternoon, a post is hammered into the ground in line with the moon as it rises above the horizon.

The moon rises slightly further to the east in each successive winter over about nine years, before slowly returning to its first position. The whole cycle takes 18.61 years. It is known as the *Metonic* cycle, after the Greek astronomer who is supposed to have discovered it, and who lived at least fifteen hundred years after the outer circles of Stonehenge were established, but all the measurements suggest that the cycle was known to the builders of Stonehenge and that the grid of posts was how they discovered it.

Well: *time*. There are six rows of posts, representing six confirmations of the cycle: that's 112 years. So for more than a century—the process handed down through generations— the yearly sighting and hammering in of posts went on. Did they take all that time to establish their basic measurement? Or did it take that long for the landscape strategy, that of using the site as an astronomical register, to be formed?

The great cathedrals of the northern plain of Europe also took hundreds of years to build, as each successive generation of masons took its place at the rock face and built its little bit. Perhaps there was an understanding that the economics of time are lost on a building intended to last forever, and built for people who speculate on eternity.

Here's another—the landscape builders of the neoclassical period planted their huge stands of trees at Versailles, say, or Blenheim, knowing that they would never see them in maturity, bequeathing the sight to their great great great grandchildren to see in a hundred and fifty years' time.

This is not a plea for lost innocence, though it might be one for lost ways of gaining experience. Everyone who's tended a garden knows how plants swallow time, and everyone knows that the oldest living things are trees. Everyone who's walked in the wilderness knows that feeling that the ground has been there forever. The lesson of these things is that it's worth spending a great deal of time on the front ends of things, getting the position right. If I asked Jean-Luc about it, he might say, "Getting things right is inevitable—with the proper time frame in place, you can see that ninety percent of our buildings are temporary anyway, yes? Just occupying the ground until the right use is found."

To which Conrad might say, to hell with all that busy building, we should be busy finding things out. "We city people should learn to allow our empty sites to lie fallow, like farmers do their fields, until we know what to do with them. We could even learn to love them in their fallow state."

Demolition

In his film *True Stories,* David Byrne comes driving down a highway in Texas in his little red convertible that looks like a saloon with the roof taken off. He smiles at the camera mounted on the film unit's flatbed truck speeding along beside him, and he says, "Some people say that the highways are the cathedrals of the twentieth century." Pause for another smile. Slightly crooked this time. "It wasn't me!"

Some people say that the highways connect the cities to each other, but do they? Is it not that they connect people living out of town to out-of-town shopping malls? Are they not the instruments of the repopulation of the countryside?

When they call you a reprobate, you may be able to reply that you are "free from convention." When they call you a mooncalf, at least you can say, "I have a lot of flesh." When they call you disillusioned, at least you can say, "I see things clearly," but what about nihilist? What can you say when they call you that? In Russia in the 1860s they watched America and Europe and Japan charging toward the modern world, and some of them saw that they would get nowhere until they destroyed the old system. Everything had to go, the old faith, the old words, the old acts and deeds. They wanted to start again from nothing. *Nihilists.* It's almost a Utopia—perhaps you could say, "At least I'm not a cynic." The nihilist program had its echo later on when, after the revolution, there was a program for decentralization that involved clearing out tracts of the cities, to spread the people out over the huge Russian landscape. Even in Britain, with one person to the acre, the emptying cities could be humanized with emptiness. We could have done it in London's defunct docklands; instead of filling it up with pointless development, we could have converted acres of dereliction to acres of parkland. We could do it in all our cities—if only we knew what the theme, what the landscape strategy for the parks created, would be.

In Turgenev's book *Fathers and Sons* the nihilist Bazarov is taken to task for his disinclination to suggest the constructive program that replaces what he would sweep away. "That is not my business," he replies, "First, the site must be cleared!"

Anyone for business?

Shed-off-the Peg

First, there is no such thing as pastiche. Everything is just what it is, good or bad in its own terms. Copying is not a problem; the quality of the copy might be. "Traveling is the ruin of all happiness!" said Fanny Burney in 1782. "There's no looking at a building here after seeing Italy." This was when all those Adam buildings were going up, looking, in comparison to their Palladian archetypes, as if they were made of solid cardboard.

About fifteen years after the Festival of Britain, about the time of *I Wanna Hold Your Hand,* there was a proposition for a building called the *Time House.* Its designer looked like a rating from HMS *Invincible,* short hair combed forward, jumper, pair of slacks, nothing to it. The Time House was a sort of family concrete bunker, in which the household of the future, unable to go outside because of the crime and the decay on the streets, stayed in and watched television. What prescience the man had! Do you recognize this? Is it already happening to you? Big locks on the door, burglar alarm on the wall, vast video library? If there's no one on the street, there's no one to look at the buildings, so the buildings don't look like anything much. It could be a concrete bunker; it could be a metal shed. With what's on the market in small commercial sheds, plus what's on the market home-defence-wise, you could set up a Time House for half the cost of a house that looks like what houses look like these days—

computer drawings of a Suffolk village—and spend the rest on machines for the inside. A shed full of machinery: perfect.

What happens next? In the next generation—perhaps one's own children's even, as they emerge from the silent, teenage years—the shed will be decorated. This sounds at first like another idea, not useless, but different, *the decorated shed*, which is that something in the ironic nature of modern life allows the architect to cover an unassuming base—the neutral entity, the shed—with iconographic shapes. I don't mean that. What I have in mind for this state-of-the-art shed-off-the-peg of yours is that the surroundings, the immediate vicinity, that is, everything within the plot boundary, will start to grow with something that is at least as good—with at least as much quality—as the devotional stonework on Notre Dame. It will take a lifetime to do it: perhaps more than one. I have no idea what yours would look like, nor you mine. Perhaps you will commission parts of it from artists. The point of the shed is that it serves the useful function while the great creative effort, the Grinling-Gibbonian work, is gradually taking shape. That's the idea of the shed-off-the-peg.

The *United Kingdom* is a crowded place. The density of population is twice that of China. The United States of America would have over two billion people in it if it had the same density. So, it's no surprise that even the wastelands are full, too. There is a spit of shingle of about thirty square miles at Dungeness, sticking out into the Channel, down there on the south coast, which is not much use for anything; so there's a nuclear power station there, a trailer park where people go for holidays, a lighthouse, the abandoned remains of experiments in radar installation, an aerodrome, and an army artillery range complete with a fake village for practicing house-to-house. There are retirement homes too, low rent, low roofed, all staring out on the cold gray sea. There are fishing shacks for keeping nets; there's a lifeboat station. All of this clutter is built on the inhospitable shingle floor, under the power pylons, in among the seakale and fish skeletons, with the gulls whirling about snatching food from each other's mouths, and the clang of the shallows warning bell tolling just offshore. In the middle of it all stands a shed of a house, surrounded by a perfect garden. The man who lives there is full of courage. His garden is made of shingle plants, more accustomed to growing wild, but cultivated here together they seem like witnesses of some sort. He's built it to be like that. The plants have fleshy leaves like cactuses and aerodynamic profiles to cope with coastal winds, and they look, when gathered together, like some exotic dream, like Xanadu in miniature. It's a minute and perfect landscape of hope in among the cast-off air of Dungeness, right in among the rubbish, and it's beautiful.

You know the little rhyme, "Sticks and stones will break my bones, but names will never hurt me?" That's not confused: there's the natural world and the moral one well separated. But sometimes people's lives get so mixed up with the world of sticks and stones that they have spilled over and become part of the landscape themselves. The stories of such lives, and the buildings they became, are extraordinary, brought about by enormous pressures, of faith, ambition, and madness, but they illustrate, in an extreme way, an idea that I have. The idea is that every building is really the conclusion of some dramatic impulse, made specific by the circumstances that surround it. The Dungeness Garden is one such place; three more are printed below: but first, I have one last confusion.

When the remains of the footings of the Elizabethan Rose Theatre were unearthed during excavations for a block of offices in London, I can remember trying to have conversations with people about authenticity. "It's just a foundation!" I said. "Why shouldn't they build on top of it?"

"But Shakespeare might have trod those boards," they said. Well—what boards? It was a pile of bricks! Shakespeare walked all over London, I expect, and all over the fields. So have I; so have millions of us. Can we monumentalize every step? If we were clearer about the quality of the impulse, perhaps felt it more, or discussed it more, or gave our lives to it more fully, committed to it more, the buildings might get stronger.

Adrian's Shrine

Adrian was a Roman soldier stationed with the thirteenth legion in his home town of Nicomedia. Part of his duty was rounding up Christians for the slaughter. He was not yet twenty, and he and his fellows thought of their prisoners as distracted people, lunatics, who met their deaths by not having the wits to renounce their god before facing the terrors of the bullring. He had seen close up many who wished they had: had seen the abrupt change in the faces of the men who emerged from the secure darkness of the tunnels leading to the arena into the dazzle of the day and who suddenly, too late, saw and smelled the bulls they were to fight.

Years later, when taking part in a campaign to put down a rebellion in Antioch, a wiser and more thoughtful Adrian, now promoted to captain, saw for himself the real thing—the bravery that faith can produce. Three brothers had been taken together as Christian agitators and forced one by one to wade through a bed of red-hot coals. The first and eldest reached halfway, until, with the embers up to his knees, his strength suddenly left him and he sank with a ghastly cry. The same happened to the second, but even so the youngest brother, having watched all this, went forward to join them. Adrian had never experienced compassion before, but now it hit him like a wave and carried him forward through the smoke and the smell of burning flesh to try and stop the sacrifice—and consequently he soon found himself under arrest, and back in Nicomedia.

Bravery was all that his new faith meant to him. He saw that his outburst of passion had not saved the brothers and had only served to condemn him. He became as stone hearted as before, but with this change: his body was now to him nothing more than a set of components through which he traveled in the present moment but which were quite separate from his real character. The dispassionate way he explained this to his interrogators alarmed them. Such a cold idea could not be explained away as superstition, and they saw that a public execution where Adrian calmly gave up the ghost would only ennoble him. Also, they were curious. Adrian's sense of identity was analogous to their own—except that they saw themselves as parts of the corporate body, and Rome as the ultimate fact: how could one exist without the other?

The tribunal deliberated and decided to undertake an experiment, to see if what Adrian said was possible. He was taken in isolation to have his limbs crushed one by one and removed. He was indeed steadfast, but his persecutors found to their relief that when the process was finished, nothing but silence filled the air.

The pieces of Adrian's body were taken and scattered with meal and piled on a fire as a public sacrifice, but at once big clouds rolled in from nowhere and a terrific storm blew up, put out the fire, and dispersed the crowd—except for a few recent converts to the faith who crept from the shadows and retrieved what they could from the pyre. His bones were boiled and cleaned, and a secret shrine was made of them, which has never been found. The children's game "St. Adrian's Church," where the fingers are made to be the church, the steeple, the parson, and the people, may give us a clue.

It is ironic that Adrian's certainty that his body was no evidence of his real existence is contradicted by the veneration of this little building of bones.

The Soanes' Family Vault

Sir John Soane, architect, 1753 to 1837, knew better than most of his contemporaries the value of a north front to a country house. The south was always devoted to garden rooms and sunlight, so it fell to the north facade to contain the entrance hall, and to be always in shadow. What with all the careful study of ruins and mausoleums undertaken by the architects of the time, any visitor approaching the gloomy, looming edifices they built was immediately cast into apprehension, as if entering a tomb. Soane actually enjoyed this feeling of "abandon hope all ye who enter here," for he felt that abandonment was liberty—that the hairs standing up on the back of his neck were excitement—that coming to grips with death in his waking hours, and toiling hard all day in its shadow, was to escape it. He surrounded himself with a huge collection of funerary items—sarcophagi, tombstones, ash urns—to maintain the proper atmosphere.

This feeling that he had attracted others of the same understanding. Notably one Robert Bourgeois, who kept the body of his dead friend Noel Desanfans in his house in Charlotte Street, in a mausoleum designed by Soane. Bourgeois arranged that on his death a museum should be built to house his collection of paintings and incorporate a new mausoleum to contain the bodies of himself, his friend, and his friend's wife. And so it came to pass. Within twenty-four hours of Bourgeois's last breath Soane was out surveying the site for the new building, paying homage to the speed with which the decision to bury the dead has to be taken.

At fourteen years old, Soane's son, John Soane junior, was taken to his father's office for the first of many fruitless and frustrating interviews. The eight years that followed were ruined by what the boy felt as a threat and the father felt as a disappointment. Soane repeatedly tried to kindle the flame of architecture in the boy, but young John, like a damp fire, refused to ignite. Their walks together in the garden, in the simulation of ancient Rome that Soane had built to inspire his son, only served to depress the boy. Even at that age, he felt that his father's predeliction for back-breakingly hard work and the collection of bits and pieces of long-dead buildings lying in the Gothick museum in the basement of the house were nothing to do with the running, jumping, and skipping life that appealed to him.

To his students, Soane was a lovable tyrant, whose greatness lit up the dark shadows of his imagination. To John and his younger brother George, he was simply a tyrant. Perhaps their mother was implicated in the little tragedy also, for when George at last made a claim for his independence by publishing a pamphlet anonymously attacking his father's work, she thought her heart would break, and indeed she died; the two young men watched as the inevitable family mausoleum was erected in St. Pancras's churchyard.

John himself died young at thirty-eight, while the old man still had fifteen years to live; so for a while his bones became part of his father's collection, laid to rest in the same vault as his mother's.

Joseph's Tondo

Joseph was born in a shed in the back garden of his bankrupt father's house in Cupertino. The baby's cries were mingled with the ring of the auctioneer's hammer in the parlor as the family possessions went under for the third time.

He grew up to be one of those vacant boys who stumble around with their mouths open, never learning to alter their stride to suit their growing height, and who forget to eat their meals, which go cold on the plates in front of them. He grew up further to be an unemployable young man: he was expelled from the kitchen of the Capuchin monastery for dropping piles of plates on the floor and then forgetting to clean up the mess. His exasperated mother eventually fixed him up as a third-level novice in the Franciscan monastery at Osimo.

It was while shoveling horse dung in the stables that his spirit gradually began to change. His idiot vacancy was filled up with rapture, to such a degree that the simple sight of a sheep would send him into ecstasies for hours about the spotless lamb of God. It was not long before reports of these events reached the head table, and the elders decided to try and turn him into a priest. Reading and writing came with great difficulty to him; in fact they never really came at all. But his disarming sense of self-denial recommended itself— no one else but Joseph could eat the disgusting mixture of wild grasses he made for his Friday meal—and it was with benign latitude that the examining Bishop decided to test Joseph on his one and only secure text, "Blessed is the womb that bears thee."

At his ordination Joseph began the most extraordinary phase of his life. All through the ceremony he floated a few inches above the floor, ravished by God's love. It used to be explained that a heart so filled with love was lighter than air, and that a levitator was a sort of human balloon. Thenceforth he spent almost as much time in the air as on the ground. The two most notable flights he made were solemnly attested to by witnesses. In one he erected single-handedly a thirty-six-foot-high Calvary that ten men had been unable to lift, and the other took place when he was due to meet a visiting admiral, who had heard that Joseph was a second St. Francis, that the sheep of the field gathered round to listen to his sermons, and that sparrows came and went at his command. Joseph came into the church where the admiral and his entourage were waiting, but as he did so his eye was caught by a statue of the Mother and Child, and he straight away became rapturous. He flew over to the statue, took the effigy of the baby in his arms, and carried it back to his cell, where he floated about with it for hours, in every conceivable attitude.

These raptures gradually turned into a proper madness. He began to frighten women on the street by throwing himself at their feet, taking them to be the blessed Virgin. One day he went into a trance from dawn to dusk. His brothers tried pricking him with needles to wake him up, and when that failed, they began to punch him. They even touched his cheeks with a red-hot poker, but he made no reaction. When he finally came to, he found himself in solitary confinement at Pietrarossa, sent there by the Inquisition of Perugia. To confirm his madness, they had built him a spherical cell, which everyone called *Joseph's Tondo*. Tondo in those days meant round, especially the round sculptured plaques the artists made, but it also meant stupid, or dumb. Deserted by men, but not by God, he spent the last seven years of his life comfortably resting against the ceiling.